Wayne Rooney

Michael O'Connell

First published in Great Britain in 2006
by Artnik
341b Queenstown Road
London SW8 4LH
UK

ISBN 1-905382-14-6

Design: Supriya Sahai
Editor: Owen O'Rorke

Printed and bound in Croatia
by H−G Consulting

Photographs courtesy:
Associated Sports Photography

Wayne Rooney

Michael O'Connell

artnik books

Blue is the colour

With his beefy physical appearance and an already-impressive glut of goals for both club and country, it's easy to forget just how young Wayne Rooney really is. Born on October 24, 1985, Wayne was still in nappies when his current club manager Sir Alex Ferguson took the helm at Manchester United in 1986. Today, a prized photo in the Rooney family household shows a cheeky young 11-year-old Wayne Rooney as an Everton mascot at the 1996 Merseyside derby, kneeling next to his own boyhood hero, Duncan Ferguson. How could anyone have guessed then that, just five years later, this would be Everton's first-choice striking line-up?

In fact, his first football coach correctly predicted, when Rooney was 9 years old, that he would play for England before he was 18! Yet, no one, not even a coach seeing such as extravagent talent for the game as he displayed at 9, could have predicted that at 20 the England manager, most of his squad and virtually all Ingerland supporters would regard Rooney as the player who could, indeed would, win us the World Cup. And when, just 42 days before the tournament started, he broke a metatarsal in his right foot in his club's penultimate league game that, as he was stretchered off, the fans would chant...

'There goes our World Cup.'

Wayne Mark Rooney was born in Croxteth, Liverpool, in the blue half of Merseyside, less than a mile from Everton's Bellefield training ground. Not surprisingly, his parents were both die-hard Everton fans and carried him along to his first Toffees game when he was just six months old. It was clear from an early age that the young Wayne was destined to be an Everton fan. Back then, Howard Kendall had built an exciting new Everton side, who had just claimed the 1984-85 league championship, beating Merseyside arch-rivals Liverpool into second place by an enormous 13 point gap. Today's giants Manchester United and Chelsea were floundering in fourth and sixth place respectively.

Growing up on a council estate in a three-bedroom house, few would have predicted that Wayne was destined for the big time. His dad – also called Wayne – was a Merseyside labourer and his mum Jeanette was a 'school food service employee'. That's a dinner-lady to you and me. Whilst Wayne never lacked for anything, the young scouser certainly wasn't accustomed to a wealthy lifestyle. It would have been even harder for anybody to imagine that the chubby young lad riding on his BMX and kicking a football around the streets of Croxteth would be earning some £6 million a year when he was 20?

Most of the children in Croxteth schools are on free school meals and many joke that young Wayne was always the first in line for second helpings. He loved nothing more than a plate of his mum's sausage, egg and chips for dinner and, if Wayne was a schoolboy today, he would certainly have no complaints about Jamie Oliver's beloved turkey twizzlers. He was often spotted down at the chippie or burger house indulging in his favourite snacks after school. Several years later, on a Manchester United team-building course in Wales, Wayne still opted for a jumbo sausage and chips at a local chippie for dinner. It was obvious Wayne was never going to let go of the culinary delights of Croxteth.

father wayne and brother

But any boy growing up in Croxteth needs to be tough. Even today, reports of police storming homes in search of armed teenage gangs and local drug dealers can be seen on local news bulletins and newspapers. Spending his youth in this tough and deprived area, it's no surprise Wayne put aside plenty of time to practise his second favourite hobby – boxing.

Rooney came from a family with a sound boxing pedigree. His father Wayne Senior was a keen amateur boxer and his uncle Richie Rooney ran the Croxteth Amateur Boxing Club, where Wayne often sparred with his brothers. 'He was very good,' Richie said later. 'He's a strong lad, Wayne.' This physical toughness and combative attitude can still be seen in Wayne today, with both good and bad results.

Sometimes we'll see it in the passionate and never-say-die footballer, who'll out-muscle anyone who tries to bully or shake him off the ball. But all too often it can erupt into those rash challenges and infamous snarling attacks on referees that have so far plagued his career. Although Wayne chose the path of football, at times it seems like those blood-splattered gloves have never really been taken off. And even if they were, underneath them are some battle-hardened bare knuckles.

But all this body-building – athletic and dietary – was soon to have its advantages. While his penchant for fatty foods ensured Wayne piled on the pounds and his boxing training toughened him up, it soon became clear that Wayne was the strongest player on the park.

From an early age, Wayne's amazing strength as a footballer was singled-out. He had been booting a ball around the streets of Croxteth as soon as he could walk and when he was just eight years old he was big and strong enough to play for a Coppelhouse Junior Under-10 side in the Walton and Kirkdale league: then, by the age of 10, he would be making appearances for the local pub side. His advanced build had been spotted by the team's trainer, John Mc Keown. 'I have a photograph of him kicking the ball at eight,' he said later, 'and you can see even then the muscles in his legs are unbelievable.'

Junior team

By the time Wayne was nine, McKeown was so impressed by Wayne's skill on the ball, as well as his strength, that he made a prediction that seemed so outlandish at the time, he felt embarrassed saying it – that Wayne would be playing for England before he was 18. 'I made the statement when he'd just turned nine, at the end of the season when we were giving out medals,' McKeown told **The Times** later. 'I felt ridiculous at the time saying it, but it's on video tape so I couldn't get away from it. There was just silence. But I meant it – and it came true.'

In a sense, it had to come true. Because football, beyond anything else, was now this kid's whole life. If football hadn't worked out, it's difficult to imagine Wayne's life without hard graft, TV dinners and pub fights. In Wayne Rooney's list of priorities, school came a very definite last – well behind football, boxing and his beloved BMX. Neighbours recall seeing his bedroom festooned with club pennants and posters of his favourite players.

Later he said: 'I wasn't interested in anything else, especially school. The only subject I liked was maths – it's the only GCSE I sat.' But long before he was even thinking of his GCSE's, the club of his dreams had taken note of his football talent.

One of Everton's scouts, Bob Pendleton, was a regular observer of the games in the Coppelhouse Under-10s league and he saw some of the incredible 99 goals that he scored in that season – it was to be his last at that level. Pendleton recommended him to Everton, but there were Liverpool scouts hovering too. Pendleton was aware that Wayne had attended 'one or two' training sessions

with Liverpool and told Everton to get in there quick. But, in truth, Rooney would rather have eaten broccoli quiche than sign for The Reds. 'It doesn't matter what they would have said to him,' Pendleton said later. 'He wouldn't have gone there. His dad, Wayne senior, also said he wasn't going anywhere else.'

All Wayne's early years were focused on football. He went through the motions of another education at the local De La Salle school, but it was clear his head was only into football. Wayne was put in the Liverpool Schools under-11s, which had also seen Everton starlet Francis Jeffers progress – as well as some famous Reds. The coach there, Tom O'Keefe, saw that he had something special on his hands. 'Wayne had such ability, he just went ahead and did his thing. We had Robbie Fowler, Steve McManaman and Francis Jeffers come through the team and Wayne was clearly every bit as good.' In fact Wayne was better – much better. He amassed 72 goals and, in his first season, broke the team's scoring record.

The same season saw the introduction of a young striker over at Liverpool in a development that could only encourage Everton. Liverpool had on their books a teenage footballer called Michael Owen who was, ironically, actually an Everton fan just like Wayne. Owen had smashed just about every schoolboy goalscoring record going and opted to play in red. Roy Evans threw Owen into the first team squad when he was just seventeen: in fact he'd got his squad number as a birthday present.

Owen was a sensation: he scored on his debut, coming on as a substitute against Wimbledon and, by his second season, became the most feared striker in England. In February 1998, at 18 years and 59 days, Michael Owen also became the youngest player to have represented England in the 20th Century.

When England travelled to the World Cup in 1998, Owen was one of the first players named in the squad in spite of his youth. As had happened with Liverpool, when they had to drop Karl-Heinz Reidle, so England manager Glenn Hoddle had to drop Teddy Sheringham, a seasoned and established international, once Owen forced his hand. He instantly contributed a goal after coming on as a sub against Romania; then a nation sat back to see him score one of the greatest World Cup goals ever in a thrilling match against Argentina.

Owen was England's youngest-ever goal scorer in a major tournament, and Wayne Rooney – not yet a teenager – was leaping from his chair along with the rest of Ingerland. Right then it was all about enjoying the moment; but most importantly for Wayne's career, a precedent was now there for teenagers to be introduced at senior levels in England. 'If you're good enough, you're old enough,' became the managerial cliché as the sport became intoxicated with youth.

At Everton, the stage was gradually being set for Wayne at club level. In October 2000, he turned fifteen and his progress ensured he was put into the Everton under-19s. Playing alongside him from time to time (though he would also be making appearances in the first team) was Wayne's older friend, Francis Jeffers, who was then one of England's most promising predatory strikers.

Rooney gets his Everton shirt

The eyes of the world were on Michael Owen. But the Everton staff knew they had the best-kept secret in British football wrapped up at their Bellefield training ground. As the giants of Europe ogled Owen and British scouts sniffed around Jeffers, Wayne was quietly developing into a striker with a range of play more exciting and telling than either of them.

In fact, back in Everton's youth team, Wayne was already playing like a Premiership striker. His repertoire was amazing for one so young. Wayne had the sort of dribbling and ball skills that could take him past two or three defenders, allied with the strength that made it almost impossible for defenders to shake him off the ball. The way he struck the ball was exemplary: he could be a lethal penalty area marksman but his shots from long range were already a threat.

The Everton staff looked on, rubbing their hands with excitement, as the young Wayne Rooney continued to develop game by game, bamboozling defenders and blasting in goals for Everton's youth team – eight in eight games in the FA Youth Cup 2001/02, including a stunner at White Hart Lane in the semis. Come the final, he tore off his shirt to reveal a vest with the fateful legend: 'Once a Blue Always A Blue.'

Rooney: no stranger to the Yellow card since his Everton days...

But little did Everton know the most successful Premiership boss in history, and manager of the most famous club in the world, was also looking on. Alex Ferguson, always keen to bring through talented youngsters, had long been in the habit of watching Manchester United youth games. One night, he just happened to be in the stands when Everton came to play. Chewing his gum ever more frantically, he looked on in horror and wonder as he saw Rooney terrorise his team's defenders and humiliate the goalkeeper with a deft chip from near the halfway line. It was rumoured that the United manager made a £5 million bid for Wayne shortly after this, although this has never been confirmed.

This same potential was being recognised by England coaches at every level. After scoring twice in four Under-15 matches in 2000/01, Wayne was then a key part of the squad at the 2002 UEFA European U17 Championship, making the kind of impact that would be mirrored in Portugal two years later: 5 goals in as many games. Then Under-17 Coach Dick Bate remembers the young Rooney well: 'Wayne had a very good tournament and in scoring five goals in five games he obviously had a major impact. He was a terrific lad in a terrific group of players and Wayne was at the soul of what made that group get on so well.'

But back at Goodison Park, Everton Manager David Moyes had his own plans for Rooney. Since his arrival at Goodison Park in 2002, Moyes had revitalised the Everton side, re-installing the talismanic Duncan Ferguson as captain – something that immediately endeared him to the Goodison faithful as well as Wayne himself.

Ferguson was a strange kind of idol, very much in the spirit of the modern Everton side: a big-time underachiever, loved by the fans without delivering the glory days. He was also Rooney's idol, with a rough-and-ready, never-say-die attitude that matched his own. With a new spirit of togetherness, Everton won three of their next four games and he saved the club from relegation. But with hardly any money to spend, it was clear Moyes was going to have to look elsewhere for the inspiration to drag his side back up the table. And, if the regular reports from his reserve team coaches were anything to go by, Moyes had a trump card that any Premiership manager would put his club in hock for.

At the start of the 2002-03 season, Moyes knew he had got something special locked up at the Bellefield Training Ground. At the age of just 16 and when most of his friends had only just taken their GCSEs, Wayne Rooney was preparing for his first season of Premiership football. Tough, strong and hungry for goals, Rooney was already the talk of the terraces. A whisper here, a rumour there was all most Everton fans knew about Rooney. But one thing was certain – this guy was special.

Fanzines tipped the youngster to national newspapers in the summer. Word had even reached an Austrian tannoy announcer: on a pre-season tour he was introduced to the crowd as 'The new Alan Shearer', and duly obliged by netting four goals in two games for the Blues in Austria. That included three against SC Weiz, the first of two Rooney hat-tricks in pre-season, and one on his debut against Bruck. By now he was regularly embarrassing the first-team players in training. As David Moyes planned his exposure to the Premiership, Wayne was like a leashed dog at the park gates.

From the first day of the campaign, Moyes made it clear that this was going to be Rooney's season. The 16-year-old striker was on the bench for the opening game against Tottenham Hotspur, and Rooney emerged from the bench to play his first few minutes of Premiership football. It was a tantalising taste for both public and player: Rooney's appetite had been whetted and he was soon given another chance to shine. Rooney was brought on for the final 30 minutes of Everton's Carling Cup game against Wrexham on October 1st 2002 and he made the park his own. By the time the game had finished, Rooney had tortured the Wrexham defence, netted two goals and become the youngest ever goalscorer in the history of Everton Football Club. Tommy Lawton's 65-year-old record turned out to be just the first of many the 16-year-old wonder-kid would break that season.

19th October Everton 2-1 Arsenal
2002/3 Premier League

A week after his cup heroics at Wrexham, Rooney had impressed as a substitute at Old Trafford, showing he could cause problems even for a top-class defence. He had been Everton's most dangerous performer in a tight game that had remained goalless until a late glut condemned the Toffees to a 3–0 reverse. But 19th October 2002 was the day Wayne Rooney announced his arrival on the big stage: the day he scored 'that goal'.

Arsenal arrived at Goodison Park as reigning Premiership Champions and FA Cup winners, on the crest of a 30-game unbeaten run. Headmasterly manager Arsène Wenger was boasting that his team of 'Invincibles' could go the whole season unbeaten. But just like at school, Wayne wasn't in the mood to listen. With the game poised at 1-1 and with just ten minutes to go, Moyes made his move. Off came Tomasz Radzinski, on came Wayne Rooney.

In the final minute of the match, when both sets of fans were beginning to settle for a point, Rooney lit the spark that would ignite his whole career. Pulling a Gravesen lob out of the air with his instep, he turned, took two paces and lashed an unstoppable strike from 30 yards over David Seaman, which clattered into the net off the underside of the bar. The Rooney sensation had arrived.

It was the first time that Wayne's old friend Francis Jeffers had been back to Goodison since joining Arsenal, and come the final whistle the man struggling to fulfil his rich promise was among the first to congratulate the boy who'd made it look easy. He had shrugged off the attentions of experienced defenders, who had just gone through an entire season without suffering what this 16-year-old had just inflicted on them: defeat away from home. The humiliated ex-England keeper shaking his head between the sticks wasn't just old enough to be his father: he actually WAS older than Wayne Snr.

The next day the papers went wild, hyping the name of Rooney onto the front pages, desperate to tell the country about this teenage scoring sensation who had only left school three months before. One ran a picture of Wayne saluting the Everton crowd with a headline 'Gunned Down' and the Gunners' manager, Arsène Wenger, was quoted saying 'The greatest young English talent I have ever seen.'

Though at just sixteen Wayne was now assured of a place at least on the substitutes' bench, David Moyes was aghast at the furore that developed around the striker. It surpassed any of the attention that was lavished on Michael Owen – even after HIS defining goal against Argentina. Football was still riding the crest of a wave in this country and interest from all parts of the media was unprecedented.

Although Wayne looked less cut-out to be glossy material than anyone since, well, Gazza, there was a new trend post-**Big Brother** for 'ordinary' celebrities in the UK. This was the year when Jade 'the pig' Goody had become Britain's biggest star, and for looks and under-class, Wayne fitted the bill. Soon a posse of press was encamped outside the three bedroom council house in Croxteth where he still lived.

It all seemed slightly surreal as the plain, humdrum facts about Rooney's life were breathlessly recounted: the fact that his tastes and leisure pursuits were barely distinguishable from most working-class sixteen-year-olds didn't seem to matter. He liked the Tiger Woods Playstation game, spaghetti bolognese, Eminem and Kanye West. His team mate Kevin Campbell, it was said, reckoned he would make a great rapper. He had dogs called Fizz and Bella, named after characters in the Tweenies. His favourite movie was **Grease** and Duncan Ferguson was the footballer he admired most – hardly earth-shattering news considering he was playing for Everton and Ferguson was the captain!

David Moyes now had to resist the constant clamour from the press – as well as the fans – for Wayne to be introduced into every game. Moyes was careful to pace Rooney, who had begun to anger senior professionals by showboating, and his manager was concerned that he developed as a human being as well as a footballer. He had noted Alex Ferguson's treatment of the young Ryan Giggs, shielding him from the full glare of the media, and cited this example as the most successful way to bring through a prodigy.

Once the fatherly Moyes had occasion to tick him off over a complaint of minor misbehaviour by a member of the public. The party line from the manager was: 'We try not to talk about Wayne, we just want to let him get on with his progress and help him all we can.' Moyes' fears that the tyro's head might be turned were prophetic but hard to guard against in practice. 'We've got to look after [Wayne], and that includes every Evertonian,' he sighed. 'If you see him out on the street send him home. I remember Sir Alex Ferguson used to offer £100 to anyone who'd tell him where his young stars were and I'm thinking of doing the same.'

22nd March Arsenal 2-1 Everton 2002/03 Premiership

As the season progressed, Wayne continued to do well while coming off the bench, scoring a series of impressive individual efforts. A fortnight after his debut wonder-goal he'd claimed another, tying the Leeds defence in knots before dispatching a low far-post strike past the despairing reach of his future England team-mate, Paul Robinson. And it wasn't only club managers who were clocking the action.

The pressure on Moyes was only intensified when the England manager Sven Goran Eriksson came out and said that he thought Wayne played too little. Could he really be thinking already of playing Wayne in the England side? Pointedly, the Scots manager said: 'If England are relying on a boy who has just turned 17 then they do have problems'.

His words rang true when England were booed off the pitch on Wayne's England debut, a February 13th friendly against Australia at Upton Park. On the day Rooney went one better than Michael Owen and became, at 17 years and 111 days old, the youngest player to represent England in any era, the team lost 3–1 at home to down-under minnows. At least Wayne played a part in setting up his pal Jeffers for a consolation goal – while Owen himself put in a poor performance.

By then Rooney's temper had already made its mark. He was red-carded for the first time in the Premiership on, appropriately enough, Boxing Day, in a 1–1 draw against Birmingham. The same day Leeds teenager James Milner broke his surprisingly briefly-held record as the Premiership's youngest goalscorer.

Eriksson clearly saw Rooney as the answer to his side's problems, not the cause, because he turned up in the Highbury stands on the 22nd March to watch Everton play Arsenal. He booked his seat, when he was told that as Tomasz Radzinski was injured and Wayne was in Everton's starting line-up.

England were soon to be facing Turkey in a crucial Euro 2004 qualifying game and Eriksson wanted some new options up front. Eriksson had become aware of the limitations of pairing Emile Heskey with Michael Owen and, for all his inexperience, Rooney was already looked a more attractive second striker. Even the Thierry Henry faithful at Highbury were keen to have a good look at the player many were calling (to David Moyes' intense irritation) 'Roo-naldo'.

Despite being allotted free-kick duties, Wayne was reduced to cameo appearances in a frustrating first half – but that was nearly enough to conjure an equaliser when his excellent work down the right produced a cross that Mark Pembridge only narrowly failed to convert. Early in the second half, Rooney set up Kevin Campbell for a shot into the side netting, but on 56 minutes the young striker finally took matters into his own hands.

Eriksson at Highbury

Picking up a pass from his veteran partner, Rooney ran ominously at the Arsenal defence and, as the hapless Pascal Cygan backed off, cracked a low shot between the defender's legs and beyond Stuart Taylor into the far corner of the Arsenal net. Parity lasted only eight minutes, though, as Arsenal were quick to wrestle back the advantage, captain Vieira ignoring the appeals to put the ball out of play for David Unsworth's injury to slam home the decisive goal. Wayne trudged off after playing a rare full ninety minutes, bitterly disappointed that his goal had been cancelled out.

But Sven-Goran Eriksson was inscrutably licking his lips. He had seen Wayne take his chance brilliantly, a mature effort against the best side in the country; furthermore, in one thrilling run during the game, he had given none other than Sol Campbell the fright of his life. Campbell was at this time Eriksson's best defender, fresh from his second consecutive World Cup as a member of Fifa's tournament XI, a man whom Michael Owen had said was the hardest he had ever played against. Eriksson had seen enough: Wayne was going to start in the game against Turkey for England, gambling on the brilliant teenager at the expense of Emile Heskey. He was to be richly rewarded.

2nd April England 2-0 Turkey 2003
Euro Qualifier

The game that Wayne found himself in was extremely tight. Turkey, third-placed in the 2002 World Cup, had held out for 75 minutes at Sunderland's Stadium of Light before substitute Darius Vassell – on for injured Michael Owen – and David Beckham turned the run of play into a richly-deserved victory, which put England top of Group Seven.

But it was Wayne's stunning competitive debut that had everyone purring, especially Eriksson who had made the biggest gamble of his career starting with such an inexperienced player. (That's if one doesn't include the liaison that he had just initiated with Faria Alam, a personal assistant at the FA, who later sold her story to a tabloid). Rooney fearlessly inspired England after the tense opening exchanges: a stunning run and pass set up Owen three minutes before half-time and he showed a mature awareness in the fiercely-fought first 45 minutes.

His aggression and skill had Turkey on the back foot from the start, and he departed to a deserved standing ovation when he was substituted. With the next crucial qualifier against Macedonia not coming up until September, seventeen-year-old Wayne could finish the season richly satisfied. His form now demanded a starting role not only in the Everton team, but amazingly also in the England team.

There were a couple of warning signs in his sensational debut season, however. Wayne managed to pick up quite a reputation among referees and other fans for the petulant side to his nature. Football is very much a game of controlled aggression and, despite no reputation for eloquence, Wayne was seen arguing with referees far too much for his own good. When the crowd taunted him, as he taunted defenders, it only wound him up even more.

His straight red against Birmingham was for a late, late challenge and Moyes, though he was furious, made no complaint about the sending off. Rooney should perhaps have learned from his opposite number, Robbie Savage, who despite his reputation as a trouble-maker plays such wind-up games that he always seems to get the other man sent off. Then again, Savage is the most hated man in the league, while Rooney is at least forgiven for wearing his heart on his sleeve. A little like a certain Paul Gascoigne.

Then, there were the personal jibes. Fans taunted him over his looks ('spud-faced') and his shape too. In fact, even an Everton chant directed at Liverpool fans wasn't exactly complimentary: 'He's Big, He's Round, He's Worth More Than Your Ground, Wayne Rooney, Wayne Rooney.' Despite his performances, it was unmistakable even to Evertonians that Wayne was hardly one for the scientific sporting diet that the majority of professional players now followed. The chips and beer that the adolescent was said to be consuming in the close season were all too evident in the physique that he presented to Everton for pre-season training.

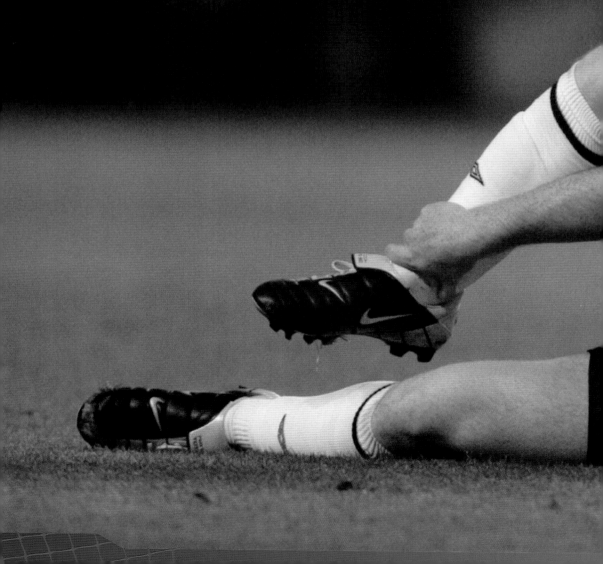

Every move that Wayne made was now being watched and some of the tabloid coverage seemed to invite the Gazza comparison. In pure football terms the comparison was a very strong one. There was the running: strong, fast, fearless, with a low centre of gravity, sublime touch and brilliant dribbling. And there was the creativity: an eye for the unseen pass, the weighted through-balls and the whipped-in crosses. Plus the ever-present threat of sensational solo goals, from rampaging runs to free kicks... in fact it seemed as though the Gazza of 1990 had been reborn but with some turbo-powered extras.

Unfortunately, part of the package was the rash challenges. The comparisons the media also loved making, of course, were in their private lives. Wayne's kebab-munching, boozing, horse-betting and, of course, his chequered domestic life were even juicier than Gazza's.

This included a love interest that has been richly documented. The romance between Wayne Rooney and Coleen McLoughlin is a soap-style fairytale, missing all the glamour that gossip columnists gorged on with the Beckhams but carrying a kind of tacky chav mythology that was almost impossible to make up. They were reported to have met up, aged twelve, when Wayne helped her to fix her bicycle. At first she turned down his advances, but when he started to get kit sponsored the footballer struck a deal with her brother, offering him a pair of football boots and shinpads if he would persuade her to go out with him.

Their first date was to the cinema followed by a hamburger. His Romeo-and-Juliet-style passion was undimmed when he found out that she came from a family that supported Liverpool, and their first kiss took place behind a local church – she was, she says almost apologetically, 'shocked at what a fantastic kisser he was'.

By the time Wayne was approaching his first (and only) full season as Everton's star striker, they were already talking about engagement and had – allegedly – celebrated the decision 'by watching **Eastenders**'.

This despite an incident from December 2002 (not reported until July 2004), where a seventeen-year-old Wayne had betrayed his relatively new love with a Scouse call-girl on a rubbish-strewn bathroom floor, two days after his sending-off against Birmingham. He might have got away with it if he hadn't signed a full confession as a memento for leggy six-footer Charlotte Glover, reading simply but touchingly:

'I shagged u on 28 Dec. Loads of Love.
Wayne Rooney.'

For now, though, Wayne's twin objectives were concentrating on getting back to fitness with a new season looming at Everton, and celebrating his 18th with Coleen and both their families in October. Once again, David Moyes was reluctant to commit the youngster too much early in the season and Wayne endured some frustrating games starting from the bench.

Moyes seemed to have the right idea, though, as Everton made a good start, staying in touch with the early leaders in the Premiership. They gained notable wins against Fulham and a 4–0 rout at Leeds which ended an Elland Road hoodoo of many years – in both cases, Wayne's considerable contributions came as a substitute. These were heady times for Everton Football Club: competing with the big boys again, the biggest talent in the country on their books, and leaving a player on the bench whom England couldn't afford to start without.

6th September Macedonia 1–2 England 2003 Euro Qualifier

At home, without Rooney, England had slipped to an embarrassing 2–2 draw against the East European republic, and were in desperate need of inspiration again in Skopje after former Barnsley striker Georgi Hristov punished a woeful first-half display to give Macedonia a deserved lead. This time, Wayne re-wrote the history books to become England's youngest scorer.

Accepting the need for the power and presence of Emile Heskey, Eriksson was tempted to haul off his inexperienced youngster. Instead he substituted Frank Lampard and bravely went for a three-pronged strike force: but it was rewarded almost instantly when Heskey nodded down Beckham's pass for Rooney to beat Milosevski from just inside the area. He was 17 years and 317 days and had once again beaten the record held by none other than Michael Owen.

It was enough to re-galvanise England and they went on to win, albeit unconvincingly. When Alan Hansen spoke about 'schoolboy, juvenile stuff' on **Match of the Day** afterwards, however, he was talking about Gary Neville and Sol Campbell, probably England's two most experienced players – not the teenage maestro who had dug England out of a hole and into Euro 2004.

Wayne was jubilant while level-headed about the prospect of playing in a major tournament. 'Scoring my first goal for England has been the highlight so far,' he said. 'You want to play against the best players to improve your game. I'm going to learn from doing that [in Portugal, not against Macedonia]. But the main thing for me is that it will be a big experience for me, something I've never done before. It will be good for my future.

'I remember watching past tournaments at home and thinking how big the games were and how nervous you'd feel going out to play in them. I never imagined that I'd be going out there playing in a tournament like that myself. Hopefully I'll be able to show how far my game has progressed.'

With an England goal in the bag now, there couldn't have been a more perfect prelude to the much-anticipated 18th birthday party that was now rather a lavish affair. He had originally planned a few beers with his family and friends in a pub in Croxteth but his agent, Paul Stretford from ProActive, hired Aintree racecourse and invited pop stars including Atomic Kitten. But as Wayne revealed, it wasn't all about self-aggrandisement so much as raising money for a local cause: 'The party will help raise money for Alder Hey. It is close to where I live and that's where I used to go as a child if I was sick. It's nice to be able to give something back.'

This was a noble sentiment in the light of tabloid attempts to 'Beckham-ise' aspects of Wayne and Coleen's life. Wayne tried to laugh off all the coverage. 'I still find it very funny some of the things that are written about me,' he shrugged, 'especially one this week that my party would be fancy dress and I was going as Oliver Hardy! That's probably been the daftest so far.'

There would be lots of snide stories like that to wind up Wayne but he was at least disguising his impatience at being on the bench well. 'I'm disappointed when I'm on the bench but I know it's for a reason and that the other players out there are doing the job. I'm still young so it's part of the learning process for me and it is the manager's decision anyway so I can't argue. My confidence has been a bit of a problem this season, mainly because I haven't scored many goals'

Though his general performances were good, there had been a lack of goals and it was difficult to see whether it was the extra pressure or David Moyes' over-protectiveness causing the slight tightening in his game. As his agent announced six sponsorship deals that Wayne had signed, he added cautiously: 'We have agreed sponsorships that are unprecedented for an 18-year-old, which David Moyes is happy about – and if he believes it will conflict with what he wants from him on the pitch, we won't do it. In fact only this week we turned down a sponsorship deal that would have been worth £3m because David didn't want him involved with that product. If all this is not managed right it will be a distraction to Wayne.'

There were, of course, other distractions in the shape of incessant transfer speculation. The lack of goals that Wayne had talked about couldn't disguise the promise he had as a player (he was still scoring for England, netting in a November friendly against Denmark) and it was reported that Manchester United and Newcastle were preparing bids for a player who had just turned eighteen. Figures around the £25m mark were already being discussed.

BROTHEL BOY
WAYNE ROONEY
HAS GOT
HIMSELF
A BRAND NEW
DEAL

FIFTY
GRANS
A WEEK
AND A
PIE
WITH EVERY
MEAL

His season had a lift on December 13th when he was called into action against Portsmouth as a first-half sub, and responded by thumping a winner which goalkeeper Pavel Srnicek could not stop despite getting a firm hand to the ball. And he was involved in a bizarre second-half incident that illustrated the other side of Wayne Rooney: after pushing over Steve Stone, Rooney walked off the pitch, apparently thinking he had been sent off, but he had only been booked and was recalled to play out the rest of the match.

Another match of his two halves came in a 1–1 draw against Leicester on 20th March. Rooney took his goal well, but his wayward idol Duncan Ferguson was setting a poor example, sent off for two violent clashes while Wayne himself received another booking – something that incensed David Moyes.

Ferguson's were not the only temper tantrums that Wayne was to see in March, however. March saw the birthday of his sweetheart Coleen and now Wayne was in a position to help her celebrate in some style – along with 200 other guests, some of whom were drawn from both of their families. There now followed an infamous 'celebration' that became front page tabloid fodder and made everyone except the participants cringe into a fetal ball.

Wayne didn't need Paul Stretford's encouragement this time to throw a huge bash for Coleen and he booked the Devonshire House Hotel in Liverpool and laid on about £10,000 worth of alcohol – as well commissioning a birthday cake that was a lifesize marzipan model of his fiancée. But it was a volatile brew. The Rooneys and the McLoughlins were seeped in the local mythology of Croxteth, with Coleen's family resented for perceived snobbery as they lived in a more lower-middle-class area on the outskirts. If the McLoughlins were unsure about the Rooneys it can't have helped to see Jeanette, Wayne's mum, drunkenly chatting up footballers and Eugene, his uncle, climbing on the tables.

At around 3 am there was an argument with the hotel staff when they closed the free bar. The shindig now turned into a punch-up, when a drunk member of the Rooney clan jabbed a finger at Coleen's mum and growled: 'You always thought you were better than us.'

In a scene straight from Harry Enfield, uncles, aunts and cousins all weighed in for a piece of the brawl. 'It seemed like everyone in the room dived into a massive scrap,' said an anonymous source. 'There were fists everywhere – and blood, bumps and scratches.' As he left the venue purple with rage, Wayne was seen by **OK!** photographers to kick and punch the wall in frustration. Fortunately it caused him no injury, but the magazine shoot became an exercise in self-parody for the proud Scousers. 'Coleen was heartbroken and I don't mind admitting I cried too,' sighed Wayne. 'Her night had been ruined.' He denied reports of a rift between Jeanette and Coleen's mum Colette, adding:

'Unfortunately because of the fame I am lucky to enjoy people think they can put the spotlight on Coleen's and my families, which is not fair on them. They are all just ordinary people who did not ask to be put in the media spotlight.'

Such tales were a green light for the tabloids to home in on 'Wayne's World' where it was perhaps the most vulnerable figure, Coleen, who was right in the cross-hairs. **The Mirror**, for instance, delighted in recounting her romps around town spending Wayne's hard-earned money. The expenses allegedly included holidays (a week in five-star Jumeriah Beach Club Resort in Dubai totalling £3000, six days in Sardinia for the same amount the next month) pets (£800 on a chow-chow dog) and a range of beauty treatments totalling £9,500 a month (manicures, pedicures, hair extensions, fake tans, facials and the gym).

At one point a spree of £40,000 in one month was reported, and it has subsequently been repeated as if it some kind of a regular monthly allowance. At that stage not even Wayne could afford to hand over such a large slice of his income just to keep Coleen off his back. Perhaps, went the speculation, he was apologising for something. Certainly every time there was some embarrassing exposé Coleen seemed to go off on a shopping spree.

Unfortunately for them, it was the beginning of Wayne and his loved one's coronation as 'King and Queen of Chav'.

Chav is sometimes said to be derived from an acronym of Council House and Violent.

Chav, recently installed in the Oxford English Dictionary for the first time, is a 21st century social group which has been broadly defined as follows: 'a subcultural stereotype of a person with fashions such as flashy "bling" jewellery and counterfeit designer clothes or sportswear, an uneducated, uncultured, impoverished background, a tendency to congregate around places such as fast-food outlets, bus stops, or other shopping areas, and a culture of anti-social behaviour.'

Take out the bus stops and some would say that it was Wayne and Coleen to a tee (especially at the **Daily Mirror**) – and, whether it was true or not, there was no stopping the tabloids. Even today a picture of Wayne Rooney, until recently our Great World Cup hope, sitting in front of a plate of chips is one of his most syndicated images.

Although tattooed Essex boy David Beckham – even Victoria calls him an 'Essex yob' – has stomached his fair share of snobbery over questions of taste, at least he and Posh were seen as glamorous new money. As yet there was little sign that Wayne was going to wear a sarong. Nonetheless, for the time being, this so-called chav with no sense of style was fair game for modestly-salaried middle-class chav-baiters.

The season ended on a disappointing note, a draw at Chelsea, with Rooney providing Everton's only spark of life in a dull match, followed by four straight Premiership defeats. They had been European contenders when the season was in its early stages but they were now finishing fourth from bottom and for Wayne it was all food for thought.

Also food for thought were the 12 bookings that he had received over the season: this was an eye-opening total for a forward to amass and clearly, Wayne had still not digested the fact that flashes of temper can turn even a great player into a liability. All his major role models for club, country and childhood – Ferguson, Beckham, Gascoigne – could attest to that. The annals of British sport were littered with talented underachievers, and Everton's more than most. Even in the last decade, Wayne was only the latest in a string of teenage striking sensations for Everton, the rest of whom had slipped into obscurity.

Michael Branch was 'the new Alan Shearer' once, an 18-year-old first-teamer described in a matchday programme from 1996 as 'the most natural goalscorer to emerge from Everton's ranks for years'; now he plies his trade at Chester City. Danny Cadamarteri, similarly, was a 17-year-old sensation whose outrageous goals provoked a row over whether he might play for England, Italy, Ireland or Nigeria. In fact, he followed Branch to the lower leagues with Bradford. And the greatest blue hope of all, the injury-prone Franny Jeffers, saw the goals dry up even before his big move to Arsenal, and he never found the confidence or will to flourish at a big club. Would Wayne stagnate in the same way if he hung around too long?

Not that any Premiership manager, nor Sven Goran Eriksson, had been put off by the actual football that they had seen Wayne play. Despite the up and down season, Wayne's performances had guaranteed him a place in England's Euro 2004 squad. The big questions being asked were how long could Everton keep Wayne – and how he would manage in a major football tournament against some of the best players in the world.

Wayne's European Tour

England's last appearance in the European Championship, when Wayne was barely into his teens, had been a hugely disappointing affair. Euro 96 and France 98 had seen a young team brimming with potential; but Kevin Keegan chose to anchor his midfield with old warhorses like Paul Ince and Dennis Wise, both 33. The highpoint of Euro 2000 was a 1–0 victory against a mediocre German side – book-ended by near-comical collapses against Portugal and Romania that saw England out at the group stages.

But there were so many contrasts between the England teams of Euro 2000 and Euro 2004. Keegan was a tactical novice, who sought to deflect accusations of being cavalier by resorting to creaking bones over callow youth: thus the untrusted likes of Rio Ferdinand and Kieron Dyer were left at home. Fast-forward to 2004 and Sven Goran Eriksson's midfield was dictated not by declining warhorses but play-making stars on the rise such as the likes of Frank Lampard and Steven Gerrard. Also, Alan Shearer had finally bowed out of international football and the Lions' attack was to be spearheaded by two generations of England wonderboys: Michael Owen, now the senior striker with 25 international goals, and the man who had stolen his thunder. 18-year-old Wayne Rooney.

13th June England 1–2 France Euro 2004 Group B

Wayne had said that the player he was most looking forward to playing against was Zinedine Zidane but he must have wished that it did not have to be their first game in the competition, at the Estadio Du Luz in Portugal.

Wayne was on a steep learning curve, but he acquitted himself well. The first half was a nail-biter as players from both teams seemed to suffer from the pre-match hype, terrified of making any mistakes. Rooney, worryingly, seemed to want to get into niggles and fights in the centre of the field. But it was England that made the breakthrough when Beckham found Lampard with a superb cross that was headed with aplomb into the roof of the net. It was the first goal France had conceded in 11 unbeaten matches.

Les Bleus came out determinedly in the second half and Rooney's raw aggression was the counterpoint to Henry and Trezeguet's artfulness. And as he grew in confidence he tormented France, who looked shaken every time he showed his power and pace. There were shades of his full debut against Turkey, especially in the 70th minute as he set off from the halfway line on another rampaging run down the left, zoning in confidently on the French penalty area with Darius Vassell in support. As Mikael Silvestre came across to cover, Wayne had two options: slip it to the unmarked man over, or take Silvestre himself on the outside. Trusting his own ability over the inconsistent Vassell, he found an extra gear and pushed it past the Frenchman. The Manchester United defender crudely hacked him down – Wayne had won a penalty.

If Wayne had passed the test of nerves, then surprisingly his much-decorated captain did not. The England talisman, who had – slightly luckily – buried one penalty against Argentina in 2002 in even tenser circumstances, had been England's spot-kick man ever since. He had held on his role despite a ghastly miss in England's last competitive game, the 0–0 return qualifier in Turkey. He got it on target this time, but goalkeeper Fabien Barthez had been Beckham's United team-mate for too long not to have a good take on where he liked to place them. Barthez read Becks' kick and saved.

This seemed to inspire a downtrodden France, as another seemingly nerveless man stepped up to change the game – unfortunately for England, it was Zinedine Zidane. With the clock running down, Emile Heskey clattered a blue shirt needlessly on the edge of the penalty area. After taking his time to assess the wall and the keeper, Zidane dispatched the ball brilliantly and France were back in the game.

The nerves were now all England's and Steven Gerrard, who had come into the tournament distracted by transfer speculation, made a calamitous back pass that left his goalkeeper, David James, one-on-one with Thierry Henry. James brought Henry down in desperation and it was a clear penalty – Zinedine Zidane emerged with the ball to place it on the spot... then in the net. This time he didn't even need to look at James.

Just minutes earlier England had looked safe; now they knew how Bayen Munich's Sammy Kuffour had felt in 1999, when he pounded the turf of the Nou Camp in despair after Manchester United had stolen victory from his grasp.

17th June England 3-0 Switzerland
Euro 2004 Group B

Wayne was learning that it was tough at the top all right and, luckily for him, he was one of the few in the team that escaped censure in the post-match inquest. Journalists from both sides acclaimed his display as the high-point of the match, possibly of the first round of games. But England's fairytale start had turned into a nightmare and the stakes were high for the next match against a Switzerland side that were meant to be no pushovers. The early signs for England weren't good as the players struggled to adapt to playing in temperatures above 30 degrees.

But, completely against the run of the play, England took the lead. The captain Beckham flighted a diagonal pass to Owen on the edge of the area: he picked out Wayne with his cross and the eighteen-year-old wrote himself into the history books with a powerful header into the far corner, becoming the youngest player to score in a European Championship. Not really known for his heading, it was some achievement and it settled England down.

Switzerland continued to pose a threat but suffered a blow when Haas was dismissed after he picked up two yellows in the space of 10 minutes. It was just an added boost to England, and to Wayne, who now enjoyed a bit of luck when he launched a ferocious shot against the Swiss goal from the left of the area. It rattled the post but it ended up in the back of the net after richocheting off the unfortunate goalkeeper.

It was **Boy's Own** stuff. Wayne was single-handedly saving England from an ignominious exit and the fans began to chant his name above all others. It was Michael Owen in 1998 all over again, only this time his famous strike-partner was barely getting a mention.

Meanwhile, his England boss was in raptures about the goals: 'He did everything...he is a fantastic talent. He played very well against France and scored two this time, one more beautiful than the other. I hope he goes on like that for the rest of the tournament, and after it. I think he'll be even better in the future. He can improve still, I'm sure about that.'

The boy wonder himself was not so lyrical in his assessment as Eriksson:

'It's a relief after the France game. We're back on track now and we've got to go on and win the next match.'

21st June Croatia 2-4 England
Euro 2004 Group B

That next match was against Croatia, who let it be known that they were very wary about Rooney. In fact, so were all the other sides in the competition who had made it through to the next round – Wayne was fast becoming the most talked about player in the tournament. European media nicknamed him the 'baby elephant', for his winningly ungainly looks and, surprise-surprise, danger on the rampage. The Croation coach singled out one of the reasons people feared and respected him: 'Rooney is a fighter, really putting in some big tackles. He is showing not just his goal-scoring abilities but also his guts and his determination.'

This was true enough, but in the next game the 'baby elephant' showed his subtler side, wrongfooting everyone again. This was one game where England started badly, going behind in the sixth minute after Niko Kovac poked the ball home. Scholes' close-range header – his first England goal in almost 30 games, dating back three years – drew England level and Wayne then struck again, latching on to a Michael Owen's pass and arrowing the ball low from long range past Butina to claim his third goal of the tournament. It was a superb strike, beating the keeper for pace into the right side of the side-netting, but his next goal showed real skill and composure too.

He was put through on goal and was facing the goalkeeper, who was coming out quickly to narrow the angle. It was the kind of situation England normally hope to play Michael Owen into, but Wayne was the man now. He took the chance brilliantly, stroking the ball past the keeper in some style. It was his best game of the tournament to date and when England went on to win 4–2, the normally guarded Eriksson gave Wayne his most astonishing praise yet:

'I don't remember anyone making such an impact on a tournament since Pelé in the 1958 World Cup in Sweden.'

And Eriksson wasn't far wrong. The tournament was finding another great talent in Portugal's Cristiano Ronaldo, but he was yet to score, while Wayne had scored two goals that were as good as anything in the tournament so far. And it just so happened that England and Portugal was the next big match in the tournament, making this a fascinating encounter between the two celebrated wunderkinds.

June 24th Portugal 2–2 England aet (Pens 6–5) Euro 2004 Quarter Final

As the game started, it was easy to see that the Portuguese defence was so wary of Wayne that Michael Owen was being provided with a lot of space to run into. It had been noted that Owen was yet to get off the ground in the goal-scoring stakes, just as he failed to score in the group stages of the last World Cup, but this was a situation that suited him perfectly. In only the third minute he latched on to a mistake by Costinha and finished expertly, flicking the ball over his head and into the back of the net. It was the perfect start but it was all to go horribly wrong for Wayne and with him England, too.

He was involved in a challenge quickly after which saw him lose a shoe. Such were the expectations of him now that it was almost a surprise not to see him shake off another two challenges and pass the ball into the goal with his sock, summoning the ghost of Gazza. Unfortunately he was clearly limping. With his strength and power, many just expected Wayne to run it off but something serious had happened and the England supporters watched aghast as Wayne was led off the pitch. The fans weren't to know but, even if England progressed, his tournament was over. The curse of the cracked metatarsal had struck again: the same injury, which had ruined the last World Cup for Beckham, Gary Neville and Danny Murphy, had screwed England again.

With this piece of good fortune, Portugal had plenty of time to make up the deficit and they began to throw everything at England. Eriksson elected to defend deeply despite three-quarters of the 90 minutes remaining, throwing on another short, pacy striker in Vassell so he and Owen could chase the same Route One balls. It offered nothing of the threat of Owen and Rooney, and as the minutes ticked by in the second half England did not do much more than hang on grimly.

The equaliser eventually came from the unlikely source of Helder Postiga, a shot-shy failure at Tottenham Hotspur with pride to play for, rescuing his whole season with a superb leaping header from the edge of the six-yard box. Suddenly roused, England poured up the other end and Campbell thought he had bagged a late winner; but just as against Argentina in 1998, his moment of glory was ruled out by a foul that the one-eyed England fans just couldn't see. In one of the most gripping finales to an international game, both teams played out extra time in something approaching a frenzy.

Portugal thought that the winner had come when Rui Costa struck a tremendous shot that came in off the crossbar, but England soldiered on. In the closing minutes, the combination of a Beckham cross and a John Terry knockdown created a point blank shot for Frank Lampard who drove the ball home emphatically: now penalties were on.

It was the England captain who stepped up to take the first penalty and, though the memory of the miss against France was fresh in some minds, no one expected him to miss. But his run of misses had cracked Becks' nerves for the big occasion spot-kicks. What he could do blindfolded on the training ground had deserted him: he was like a champion golfer who suddenly couldn't putt anymore. He struck the turf awkwardly in his run up to the ball and, then, wellied over the bar.

Vassell repents

All Portugal had to do now was to score their penalties but they still managed to miss one and, as the shoot-out went to the death, it was an England player who made the next mistake. As the England sub Darius Vassell prepared to take his spotkick, the Portugal keeper Ricardo took off his gloves and theatrically chucked into the back of the net. Vassell drove a half-decent penalty low to the keeper's left but Ricardo had guessed right... he saved it. Ricardo then took the next spotkick and scored. England were out.

Why did Ricardo take off gloves that crucially enhance a keeper's grip? He explained later: 'I had to do something different after not standing a chance for the first three penalties.' It was a kind of subliminal message to Vassell: I can beat you with my bare hands.

Eventually with two even sides penalties come down to nerves, psychology and luck. Ricardo made his own luck.

In the event, many were disappointed with England's showing in these finals. They had been one of the favourites but went out in the last 16, which even though they had been beaten by a very good Portugal side on their home turf meant they hadn't lived up to their billing. But, for all England fans, the solace came in the fact that they had in Rooney the star of the tournament. Officially, he wasn't the player of the tournament at all as he had only played in three-and-a-bit games but he was the talk of the tournament. He had scored as many goals as Ruud van Nistelrooy who played more games and was a specialist target man-cum-poacher.

It was an incredible achievement that was not lost on some of Europe's biggest clubs who saw these kinds of tournaments as a shop window for future star players. As Wayne headed back to Everton for rehabilitation after his injury, he was tight-lipped about the chances of him staying at Everton while the club were voluble in expressing their desire for him to stay.

Rooney delights fans with his trademark cartwheels...

A New Era

There were certainly moves afoot in the transfer market, even before Euro 2004 reached its surprise conclusion (defeat for the hosts at the hands of Greece). Not surprisingly, in the case of Rooney, the big European clubs decided to hang fire rather than sign a teenager for a world record fee. Real Madrid were quoted as saying they would move for him eventually, perhaps after the next big tournament. Yet, in a roundabout way, it was to be a signing by Madrid that determined Wayne's future.

Real Madrid were going on their annual spending spree and with an aging back four being broken up, they splashed out £13.4 million on Newcastle's Jonathan Woodgate. Newcastle were eager to show the expectant fans that the sale reflected no loss of ambition and, in a deliberate PR move, made it clear that with these funds they could make a serious offer for Wayne... should he become available. At this point not many people believed that the 'True Blue' would even consider leaving Everton and David Moyes or that Everton would dream of letting him go. The faithful were in for a big shock.

In the modern game, sentiment only figures in the rhetoric propogated for fans and the media, what really matters is the figures in the balance sheet. This applies to both club and player. Increasingly, given the money in the game, top players are like medium-sized companies with a board of agents, managers and lawyers advising them on how to maximise the profitability of their assets. In this respect they become no different than the clubs they play for. The big difference, of course, is that a player's shelf life is much shorter.

A team like Everton is ideal for a promising player to cut his teeth but offers little hope of playing for major trophies; whereas at a club like Arsenal, which does the tournament circuit, such a player might not get a game. At this point in his career, Rooney had more than cut his teeth but he was also at a club where a long-term dearth of silverware had taken its financial toll. And even with a Rooney, Everton could still be looking at a future of sustained mid-table football.

Wayne, of course, WAS something special. Everton's biggest asset had given them a rare chance to make a difference. The club now faced a dilemma: rely on a teenager to drag their fortunes single-handedly upwards on the pitch or cash in while his stock was at its highest? The fans still hoped for the fairytale but Sven-Goran Eriksson had clarified the bottom line by putting Rooney onto the big stage where he had delivered. The transfer market would now make the running. Both the club and Rooney plc knew that a single word from either camp could mean a big pay-day for everyone involved.

In such a case, the onus is on the player to decide and Wayne did: it was really a no-brainer. In August 2004, Wayne held talks with David Moyes and then made the following announcement:

> *This has been one of the hardest decisions of my life [he was still 18] but I feel the time is now right for me to move forward with my career. The Euros were a fantastic experience for me. It made me realise I could play at the highest level. To do that I need to be with a club that is playing in Europe every year. I hope the Everton fans can come to understand my decision and I hope the transfer fee Everton Football Club receive will help the club move forward. The Everton fans have always been fantastic in their support of me. I hope they respect my decision and I also hope that some day in the future I could be welcomed back to watch the team I have supported since boyhood.*

While the fans went into mourning the statement from David Moyes and the club was actually quite business-like: 'We are disappointed, but at this time he is an Everton player and will remain that until we receive what we think is his valuation. We have got a fee in mind but we won't be discussing what it is. Until we get our valuation there will be no movement. He's a player we value really highly. We showed that by the effort we put into his [£50,000 a week] contract offer.' Moyes also added: 'I'm not sure this would have happened if Newcastle hadn't sold Jonathan Woodgate'.

This meant that Newcastle were almost certainly going to be bidders if Wayne wanted a transfer. But who were going to be the real contenders? There could only be two: Chelsea and Manchester United. Chelsea were currently installing José Mourinho as manager and the club, bankrolled and owned by billionaire Roman Abramovich, had given him an open cheque to buy any player he wanted. Mourinho knew about Rooney – he'd been a TV pundit during Euro 2004 – but he had just bought Didier Drogba for £24 million and he felt Rooney was still too young to splash out on. And like Wenger he wasn't keen on home-grown domestics, preferring continental or South America stock.

This meant that realistically it was only United who were in the running. Alex Ferguson had not forgotten Wayne, of course: the kid in the youth game who had pulled off that audacious chip from the half-way line. At the time Ferguson was struggling to remould the Manchester United team after years of almost uninterrupted success. He was faced with the challenge of both Chelsea and the new 'Invincibles' of Arsenal, and was going to require something special to start winning back his trophies.

With Cristiano Ronaldo, the other young star of Euro 2004, already in his squad, the idea of having Wayne in the squad was an audacious one and would be highly popular with the fans. The truth is, however, that like all the other European giants Manchester United had been content to wait for Wayne to spend another year or two being polished up before they put in a bid. Ferguson had just bought Alan Smith from Leeds and Louis Saha from Fulham, and really he needed midfielders before he brought in another striker.

However, the prospect of Newcastle taking the initiative and snatching him from under Fergie's nose – as they had with Alan Shearer in 1996 – was more than he could stomach but it was the imperative of success that forced United's hand. As Ferguson put it:

'I've known his potential for a long time, but the way he has played in the last three years has been phenomenal. We could not afford to miss him.'

Initially, Manchester United played it cool and simply matched Newcastle's offer of £20 million, thinking that the prospect of playing for a regular Champions League team would be enough to tempt Wayne. There should have been no surprise when this was flatly rejected by Everton and both clubs had to go back and think of another number.

The background to all this was intense disquiet in Liverpool at the move but Sir Alex Ferguson was already talking about Wayne as if he was a Manchester United player. Ferguson said: 'It only takes a second to say yes. The difficulty is getting the medicals but at the moment it is not at the stage where we are talking about it. We are waiting for an agreement before doing anything else. Rooney's a fabulous player – he showed that at Euro 2004 – and is a young player. He's not the finished article yet, but we've got experience of bringing young players to the club and bringing them on.' Yet the United board were unaware that Wayne had already set his sights on the Manchester club from the moment they came into the frame.

Rooney get his Man U shirt

The deadline for transfer completions was fast approaching and Newcastle made a last effort to tempt Wayne and Everton with a £23.5 million bid. But with debts amounting to £30 million, Everton were happy to hold out for more and confident that Manchester United would take an even bigger plunge. They were right about United because the club upped the ante run to burn off Newcastle. But they let Everton sweat a bit by not bidding until they were right up against the transfer deadline.

Manchester United completed the signing of Wayne Rooney on the evening of August 31st, in a deal worth £27 million. They paid Everton a guaranteed £20m, with that sum rising by as much as £7 million according to the 18-year-old striker's appearances and achievements. Those achievements, including European silverware and England caps, were seen as bankers by both sides, a kind of guarantee of United's success in the Rooney era. Wayne's salary went up to £50,000 a week – just a couple of years before Everton were giving the schoolboy £100 a week. Wayne thought he had signed with football, not pound notes, at the forefront of his thinking. 'I'm excited to be joining a club as big as Manchester United. I feel this can only improve my career,' he said. And his value too. The balance sheet had spoken.

The blue half of Merseyside does not listen to balance sheets nor, for that matter, in this case did the red half. Liverpool were not exactly over the moon at seeing such a player going to their other biggest rivals. The fanbase, of course, is where the sentiment is concentrated and it reacts emotionally.

The hate-mail poured in to new Everton chairman Bill Kenwright – friends said he was 'devastated' by the transfer – and to Wayne's agent Paul Stretford, who was known to advised Wayne on his move. Proactive Management were forced to issue a statement on the matter, condemning the 'misguided individuals' responsible and insisting that Wayne had backed his agent every step of the way. For this reason, the wrath of the heartbroken Everton fans now descended upon the player himself.

If this wasn't enough to take the shine off the beckoning silverware, it was further tarnished by some more juicy tabloid revelations. In a story that was more farcical than it was sordid, it was reported that Wayne had frequented a sleazy back-street brothel in Liverpool – again even signing autographs as he stood in the waiting room of the dingy establishment. On another visit, despite being warned that the police were about to stage a raid, he was said to have fallen asleep on a sofa. It seems he had visited the brothel at least eight times, around 18 months before, having sex with a number of pros including a mother-of-six who dressed as a cowgirl and, notoriously, a 48-year-old grandmother who wore a rubber suit. 'Don't Fancy Yours Much Wayne,' howled **The Sun** as it ran a picture of the harried-looking granny drawing on a fag.

The revelations put a new strain on the player's relationship with Coleen, coming just weeks after call girl Charlotte Glover spilled the beans on her romps with Rooney. Coleen decided it was time to go shopping again – this time to New York's Macey's with a couple of her mates in tow.

Wayne's agent decided another public statement on his behalf was called for:

'Foolish as it now seems, I did on occasions visit massage parlours and prostitutes. It was at a time when I was very young and immature and before I had settled down with Coleen. I now regret it deeply and hope people may understand that it was the sort of mistake you make when you are young and stupid.'

The couple went into hiding for a while, with Coleen going on shopping sprees as she came to terms with these revelations. Some reports in the more uncharitable tabloids suggested that it more her cashing in rather than shopping therapy. Meanwhile Wayne was desperate to get himself in the papers again for his football – as well as wanting to save the relationship. Sadly it was inevitable the row was going to be public. Coleen 'felt dirty', friends told the press.

Amused newspaper reports suggested that after the first scandal broke she had hurled her £25,000 diamond and platinum engagement ring into the trees at Formby Point, a squirrel reserve. **The Sun** described how hordes of opportunistic Scousers were piling into the nature sanctuary with metal detectors to bag the prize. Stories of 'Auld Slapper', apparently a footballers' regular although she later sued for defamation, were even more embarrassing. The timing couldn't have been worse, on his first season with a new club, and Rooney was well aware that the fans on the terraces would be merciless with their chants. He had a stay of execution as he was still recovering from his summer injury when the transfer was completed; but as soon as he was playing for United, he would have to play out of his socks to shut people up.

With the football calendar starting in mid-August, it was a long and frustrating wait for Wayne till the end of September, when he was cleared as being fit to play. After coming through a few reserve games with no problems, he was delighted to find that he would be making his debut not in the Premier League but in the Champions League, against Turkish side Fenerbahce.

28th Sept Manchester United 6–2 Fenerbahce
Champions League 2004/05

The Champions League is the benchmark for a football club with pretensions to quality. The ban on English clubs after the Heysel disaster left teams lagging behind in Europe and as of 2004 Manchester United were the only club from these shores to have won the tournament since the restitution. First-time players, no matter how experienced elsewhere, can find it takes many games to acclimatise to the standard of competition. It was going to be a baptism of fire for the eighteen-year-old, but Alex Ferguson remembered how well the tyro had done in his surprise selection against Turkey for England. Still, not even his own fan club would have predicted the kind of debut that he was going to make.

All eyes at Old Trafford were on the England striker as he took to the field, all hugely aware that he had not kicked a ball in a top class competitive match since limping out of England's Euro 2004 quarter final defeat to Portugal. So, there was a little ripple of excitement when he produced a stylish lay-off for Bellion on the right only for the Frenchman to produce a poor cross into the area.

In the absence of Roy Keane and a number of other senior players, this was no walkover for United. But on 7 minutes Ryan Giggs found Kleberson on the left wing, who bided his time before whipping in a precision cross for Giggs to glance low into the left-hand corner. This early goal settled any United nerves and paved the way for Wayne to turn it on.

United went on a counter-attack and worked the ball to van Nistelrooy, whose defence-splitting pass found Rooney hurtling towards the left-hand side of the box. There was a gasp of anticipation – would he bottle it? – but he answered emphatically with a stunning left-foot finish from just inside the area that positively flew into the roof of the net, beating Rustu Recber at his near post. It was a perfect start for Wayne Rooney and the cheers were deafening, but no-one could quite believe it when he followed this with a mazy run and a thumping shot into the bottom right hand corner.

This time it was hard, low and across the goalkeeper from just outside the D – a perfectly contrasting companion-piece to his first goal. It was worth bearing in mind that the unfortunate Rustu was one of Europe's best keepers: he won the golden gloves plaudits at the 2002 World Cup.

Fenerbahce reduced the deficit after the restart when Nobre capitalised on poor defending to send Alex's corner past Roy Carroll. Goal difference might yet be a factor in the group, so when United won a free kick soon after the Fenerbache goal the fans hoped a recognised free-kick taker like Ryan Giggs might restore their cushion. As new-boy Wayne waved away his team-mates and prepared to take the 25-yarder – it looked like he'd usurped the designated set-piece specialist in order to complete his hat-trick – one half-expected to Fergie to come raging down the touchline and demand to know what was going on. With one look at his target, Wayne stepped forward and curled an exquisite free kick round and over the wall and beyond the despairing lunge of Rustu. It was a free kick that made light of David Beckham's absence and the fans nearly lifted the roof off as they chanted Wayne's name. It was an extraordinary **Boys Own** debut: a hat-trick for Manchester United in the Champions League!

The game became a bit of a formality after this and the game ended with Wayne and Ruud van Nistelrooy combining to great effect in the rest of the game. Alex Ferguson's smile had never been so broad when he was asked afterwards if he had ever seen such a debut before: 'I don't suppose so,' he said, with some understatement. 'It is a great start for him. That's why we signed him. He is only a young boy, don't forget. He obviously tired in the last 20 minutes, but given that it was his first game since the European Championships you could expect that. Given that Wayne and Ruud played together for the first time the future holds great promise. I think he can only get stronger.'

The idea that Wayne could get better was frightening for the rest of the Premiership. Ferguson added: 'The important thing for me as a coach is to allow the boy to develop naturally without too much public attention. I want him to be as ordinary as he can.' All this told the world was how extraordinary a footballer Ferguson actually thought Wayne Rooney was. The opposing coach Christophe Daum summed it up magnanimously too (he was something of a kindred spirit, having also suffered a high-profile hooker scandal). 'Rooney is still very young and maybe he will become the player of the century,' he concluded. And one of the players of the last century, and a Manchester United legend to boot, was also queueing up to join in the praise.

The one and only George Best, seen beaming from the stands, eulogised: 'You look at that performance and you have to say that's as good as anything you've ever seen. He's got to maintain that level of performance but there's no reason why he shouldn't.

'He's got everything going for him, he's looking the complete player at 18 years of age.

'He can handle himself, he has two good feet, he's good in the air, he's got it all.' It was certainly the case that we'd just seen a truly complete hat-trick: left-foot, right-foot, set-piece. Best continued:

'You go through all the greats at Manchester United and you've certainly got to put him in there.'

George Best

From someone who was notoriously sceptical about pretenders to his throne, this was the highest possible praise and capped everything for Wayne. With George Best's approval he was, officially, a Manchester United legend after just one game. There was one word of warning from the great playboy though: 'His main objective away from football will be to keep off the front pages.'

24th Oct Manchester United 2-0 Arsenal
2004/05 Premiership

It was now time for Wayne to get down to Premiership business, and another big game beckoned against Arsenal at Old Trafford. It just happened to be the game where the champions Arsenal going for their 50th match unbeaten – and it just happened to fall on Wayne's birthday. This was already set to be a controversial encounter because of the bad blood spilling over from the previous season's 'Battle Of Old Trafford', where the game had nearly descended into a mass brawl. United had seen their bitter rivals not only take the title but also win without losing a single game. To a man and a manager they were determined that Arsenal's run was going to end on 49.

As always, it was a tense game and the first half was goalless, though Wayne came closer than anyone to scoring. Arsenal midfielder Patrick Vieira had just about passed a fitness test to make the team sheet but an early clanger suggested he should have stayed on the bench: he let a pass slide under his foot and almost gifted Rooney a goal but Kolo Tourè flung himself to block his shot. When Paul Scholes gathered the rebound and again played in Wayne, he cut the ball back this time to an unmarked Ryan Giggs. Giggs struck the shot well only for some more desperate Arsenal defending to come to their rescue, with Campbell managing to get in the way of the strike. Even with their raucous home support, it was going to be difficult for United to break down this Arsenal side.

Worryingly for United, after the interval it was Arsenal who came out with their tails up. Dennis Bergkamp and Thierry Henry were denied by good saves from Roy Carroll. Arsenal were then left bewildered when the referee ruled against a penalty after Freddie Ljungberg went down under Ferdinand's challenge as he raced on to an Edu through-ball. The attack served as a warning to United as Arsenal started to get their free-flowing passing game into gear.

United's response was to work the ball to Rooney, who found space in a dangerous spot on the right hand side of the penalty area, looking to cross with Sol Campbell breathing down his neck. Wayne changed direction suddenly as he tried to turn the ball away from Campbell and, all of a sudden, it looked like the defender's trailing leg had brought him down. To this day, Campbell maintains that he didn't touch Wayne and the TV replays certainly back him up. He was incandescent... while Rooney was already wheeling away in triumph at the penalty decision. With the Arsenal players still protesting, it was van Nistelrooy who stepped forward to take the penalty. The Dutchman, who had missed at 0–0 in this fixture the year before, calmly dispatched the spotkick into the net and with not long to go Arsenal chased the game for an equaliser.

The away team surged forward leaving too many gaps at the back and soon United had seized on a mistake and broke away on the counter. With too many Arsenal players committed, they found themselves outnumbered and the ball was worked to Wayne who had a simple slot home from six yards to make United winners – the perfect birthday present. Not that Arsenal were going to sing 'happy birthday' after seeing him unfairly blow out their candles.

Campbell and Rooney were still slagging each other off as they went down the tunnel to the changing rooms. Wenger was going on about how van Nistelrooy 'cheats' and moaning about United's physical game. Ferguson started shouting at him to shut up and take his loss like a man: unusually for Wenger he squared up to him. Fergie eyeballed him down. A couple of the Arsenal subs, who were already in their changing room, picked up some of the interval refreshments and threw them at Fergie. The 'Battle of the Buffet' as it became known had been joined. Fergie ended up with pea soup on his suit and shirt. As is his habit on occasions when Arsenal are under investigation, Wenger reached for his white stick: 'I don't know about food throwing. I did not see if something was thrown.' By all accounts, it was instigated by 17-year-old Cesc Fabegras, who'd stayed on the bench. Thankfully, no one had a handbag to throw... not even Ashley Cole.

17th November Spain 1–0 England International Friendly 2004

This petulant display from senior international players did not perhaps set the best example of sportsmanship for Wayne as he prepared for his next game with England, a friendly at the Bernabeu. In the event, Wayne was feeling far from friendly on what was meant to be England captain Beckham's big day.

The game in Madrid's ground was the most febrile atmosphere that Wayne had experienced since Euro 2004, only made worse by the racist chanting that could be heard from some quarters of the Spanish crowd. This followed the Spanish manager Luis Aragones' 'piece of black shit' put-down of Arsenal's Thierry Henry to motivate one of his own players, Jose Antonio Reyes (also of Arsenal). This was another one of those games where England were outclassed technically but unusually were unable to stamp down on the skill with their trademark mixture of pace, aggression and teamwork. All this added to the frustration of England's

But no-one could fathom what was going on in Wayne's mind. With just 12 minutes on the clock, he lunged at Spain's Joaquin, a brutal challenge that threw the Spaniard right up in the air. It also happened right in front of the referee but, presumably because it was a friendly, no card was produced. However the bull elephant was on the rampage. Next Wayne decided to contend a ball, even though it was lost cause, with Spanish keeper Casillas. He charged into Casillas bulldozing him off the ball and into the advertising boards. The Spanish side side coulnd't believe it: it was a friendly for christsakes. One said later that while they were remonstrating with Wayne 'there was nothing in his eyes'.

Beckham (not for the first time) pulled Wayne away from trouble after the yellow card was flourished, but the scouser reacted like a school prefect had tried to stop him beating someone up in the playground. He turned on Beckham with a vollery of abuse that was as venomous as it was unbalanced. Beckham knows when discretion is the better part of valour – he kept trying to defuse and placate. But no one had a clue why England's star forward was running amok. Sven Goran Eriksson probably didn't need the signal from Beckham to take Wayne off, he had seen enough already and hauled the teenage forward off with only 42 minutes gone. There were shades here of Gary Lineker's signals to the bench when Gazza lost it in the 1990 World Cup semi-final.

But worse was to come. The England players had been playing with black armbands to mark the passing of a former England and Liverpool captain, Emlyn Hughes, and once Wayne realised he was being replaced by team-mate Alan Smith, he tore his off and threw it on the ground. Like fuck Liverpool. It was meant to be his grand arrival on the Spanish stage, but that night he'd struggle to get himself bought a drink in Madrid, let alone sell himself as a future galactico. His actions were even less well received back home and he was on the front pages as well as the back.

That night in Spain, more than any comic stories about family punch-ups and geriatric hookers, presented serious concerns about his ability to fulfill his potential, to fans and coaches alike. He did nothing positive on the pitch but much worse showed himself to be a liability to his side when the chips were down. Alex Ferguson has vowed to calm down Wayne Rooney – but without diluting his competitive edge. 'Players want to kick him and at 19 he'll react to that,' he said. 'In two or three years he won't because he'll let his feet do the talking. We'll settle him down, don't worry. But Wayne won't be bullied by anyone.'

Despite the defence there was, still, a worried edge to Ferguson's comments as he knows full well that if the tough nut in Rooney isn't cracked it could ruin his football career. He also offered in mitigation the fact that Wayne had apologised to his England team-mates for the outbursts in Madrid.

It was reminiscent, too, of David Beckham having to apologise to team-mates for getting himself sent off against Argentina in 1998. Beckham was demonised after this and had to go into media rehab. But unlike the public witch-hunt that summer, people knew that in Wayne they were dealing with someone who if he wasn't good at football would be more likely to be serving time at her Majesty's Pleasure. Wayne really could help his upbringing and background: allowances had to be made. Nothing put this in greater relief than when he spoke in public. It was painful.

After his first season with Everton he had received the award for BBC Young Sports Personality Of The Year, when he collected the trophy he was chewing gum and completely himself. It was like Gazza but without even an attempt to cover up the inadequacy with jokes that don't work. At the time, his father had said simply, 'It's what he does on the pitch that matters' and Wayne set about proving that maxim. In fact, as Ferguson began to let him talk a little more in carefully-vetted interviews, he would reveal himself as a reasonably articulate and thoughtful young man. So long as he stuck to football, anyway.

14th Nov Newcastle 1–3 Manchester United 2004/05 Premiership

Though Manchester United were already slipping behind in the title race with Chelsea, Wayne was beginning to make a case for being one of the most exciting players to watch in the country. He scored twice against Newcastle in a thrilling game at St James' Park that really got United's season going. Alan Shearer and Patrick Kluivert went close for Newcastle before Rooney volleyed home brilliantly to stun the home crowd in the seventh minute. Darren Fletcher, wide on the right flank, picked Rooney out in space but the 19-year-old still had plenty to do: he demonstrated fantastic technique and confidence by turning to rocket the ball first-time past Shay Given. Shearer eventually levelled the scores with a fine individual goal after dispossessing Wes Brown but Ruud van Nistelrooy scored from the spot after Shay Given fouled Paul Scholes. Rooney had the final say, slotting home from close range to seal victory in the closing seconds. The volley was the talking-point, although it wasn't even to be Wayne's best effort against Newcastle that season.

It wasn't just his goals but his all-round play that was impressing. But just a month later when Manchester United met Bolton at Old Trafford, Alex Ferguson found himself defending Wayne again. His manager insisted he did not deserve to be sent off after appearing to shove his hand in Bolton defender Tal Ben Haim's face. The incident was missed by referee Dermot Gallagher, so he remained on the field. But where Wayne was concerned the media were now doing the referee's job for him. Even though he was playing out of his skin, the media were constantly blowing the whistle.

15th Jan Liverpool 0–1 Manchester United
2004/05 Premiership

The next month Wayne proved again that he was not the kind of player who would hide in the big games. United were playing Liverpool at Anfield: one of their biggest games of the season against the team who would be crowned European Champions under Rafael Benitez.

United had suffered injury setbacks when Alan Smith and Rio Ferdinand were ruled out, while Ryan Giggs was still absent with a hamstring problem, so they were on the back foot even before the kick-off. Liverpool dominated the early stages, but were stunned on 21 minutes when United were gifted the lead by Liverpool goalkeeper Jerzy Dudek – with a little help from the boy wonder. Rooney cut in from the left and tried his luck from 25 yards. Dudek appeared to have it covered but somehow let the powerful shot slip behind him into the net, and it was good enough to win the game for United. It was reward for Wayne's have-a-go attitude and vicious striking of the ball, but when Wes Brown sent off for two bookable offences with half an hour to go the striker showed his resilient side, helping to cover his defence against Liverpool's remorseless search for an equaliser. Still, he picked up a booking for taking a kick at Luis Garcia after the Spaniard's strong tackle in a match that was played almost at boiling point.

Another positive contribution came in the same month against Aston Villa, where Wayne showed his more unselfish side as a player - and his blossoming partnership with Portugal's answer to him, Cristiano Ronaldo. Early on the two seemed reluctant to pass to each other; here they were the architects of this success, United striking twice inside a minute to finish the game as a contest.

Ronaldo tackles Finnan, ManU v Middlebrough FA Cup 2004

Wayne had been tormenting Villa on the wing all afternoon and, with the scores level, scampered away down the right before crossing beautifully for Saha to divert the ball goalwards, a deflection off Liam Ridgewell helping the ball past a wrong-footed goalkeeper. Moments later Ronaldo's trickery earned him an opening and his stinging drive was parried into the air by Sorensen for Scholes to nod into an empty net.

Unfortunately for United, though, their chance of winning the Premiership were long gone, instead they were locked in a battle for second place with Arsenal – as well as on collision course with them in the FA Cup. Their progress in the cup had been slowed by an embarrassing draw against Exeter at home where Wayne had not played, but Ferguson brought him and Ronaldo into the side for the replay and both scored to seal passage into the next round, a game against Middlesbrough.

Jan 29th Manchester United 3-0 Middlesbrough FA Cup 4th Round 2004/05

Now Wayne produced two wonder goals that turned out to be the highlight of United's run in the competition. United made a flying start and went ahead after 10 minutes, with O'Shea firing powerfully into the top corner past Schwarzer after Middlesborough struggled to clear. The Middlesborough keeper had a fine game but was powerless to prevent Wayne doubling the United advantage with a brilliant individual goal after 67 minutes. Gary Neville released the teenager, who spotted Schwarzer advancing off his line and delivered an audacious chip from 40 yards, clipped with the dexterity of a golf shot but delivered on the run.

He provided another piece of magic after 81 minutes to crown an impressive United display: Louis Saha flicked on Carroll's clearance and Rooney met it with a stunning volley on the turn that flashed high past the diving Schwarzer. Alex Ferguson purred: 'The first goal was precision... they were both marvellous goals.' Meanwhile the Boro manager Steve McClaren, familiar with the player in his capacity as England No.2, added: 'In Wayne Rooney they had the difference on the day. He is a magnificent player.'

The FA Cup continued to prove a happy hunting ground for Wayne as he made a winning return to Everton in the quarter-finals. He received a hostile reception from his old fans and he was even involved in an angry exchange with a spectator before kick-off. But goals in each half from Quinton Fortune and Cristiano Ronaldo went a long way to silence the jeers at Goodison Park, though Wayne's every touch was met with a deafening chorus of boos from the crowd that once idolised the 19-year-old. Everton had been performing remarkably well in Rooney's absence, but they still lacked the class he provided up front.

26th Feb Manchester United 2-1 Portsmouth
2004/05 Premiership

The disappointment of not scoring at his old ground was allayed by another glorious Premiership performance, as he scored twice against Portsmouth. He gave United an early lead, deftly diverting Gary Neville's cross past Pompey's Konstantinos Chalkias and then latched on to Ruud van Nistelrooy's pass with 10 minutes left and superbly slipped the ball past Chalkias again from eight yards. Once more, his boss was effusive in his praise: 'Wayne Rooney was fantastic. He was by far our best player – absolutely magnificent. Wayne picked up the baton for us and ran to the line. He was on song for us throughout the whole game.'

But this all hid some frustration at Old Trafford. Ferguson was doing what he could to talk up United's hope for the future as they had just gone out of the Champions League against AC Milan. It was another depressingly early exit, albeit in a tight game to the eventual finalists – but Wayne had enjoyed little space to shine against the legendary Rossoneri defence. The highlight of their whole European campaign was still Wayne's dazzling performance in the Fenerbache match. Still, his personal tally in all competitions was now 15 goals in 33 games, a fine return for a player who Ferguson was playing as a withdrawn striker or even sometimes on the right or left of midfield... and there were still a lot more goals to come than this 15.

He was becoming, in particular, Newcastle's worst nightmare as he defied injury to score another memorable goal against them at Old Trafford. It triggered a fightback after a terrible run of form had seen the team lose their last two and register only one goal in six league games – their worst goalscoring run since December 1989. Newcastle had taken a surprise first-half lead but Rooney's brilliantly-executed volley, hit with the outside of his right foot on the gallop from 25 yards, drew gasps from the Old Trafford crowd.

With time running out, Wes Brown's winner provided a bigger surprise (it was his first goal in 117 league games), but the first goal was the main talking point of another exciting game between the two teams. In a rare interview, he then went on to warn that he wanted to score even more:

'I was happy to get another goal but I think I can do better. Hopefully next season I will do.'

This is what he told MUTV (United's own local TV channel) before the FA Cup final against Arsenal. He added: 'We want to win all our games going into the final. April was a bad month for us but we have got back to winning ways and we need to keep it going. The Cup final is going to be massive for everyone. We will all be trying to keep fit so we can fight for our place.'

But there was no need for Wayne to fight for his place and it was a hugely important day in his young life. The Millennium Stadium gave him the ideal platform to showcase his genius with a prize awaiting him at the end, which would be his first senior trophy. With the Premiership and the Carling Cup already lost to Chelsea, and Liverpool contesting the Champions League final with Milan, it was the only chance left to him that season. Plus of course, Wayne's first FA Cup winner's medal was the stuff of every lad's boyhood dream.

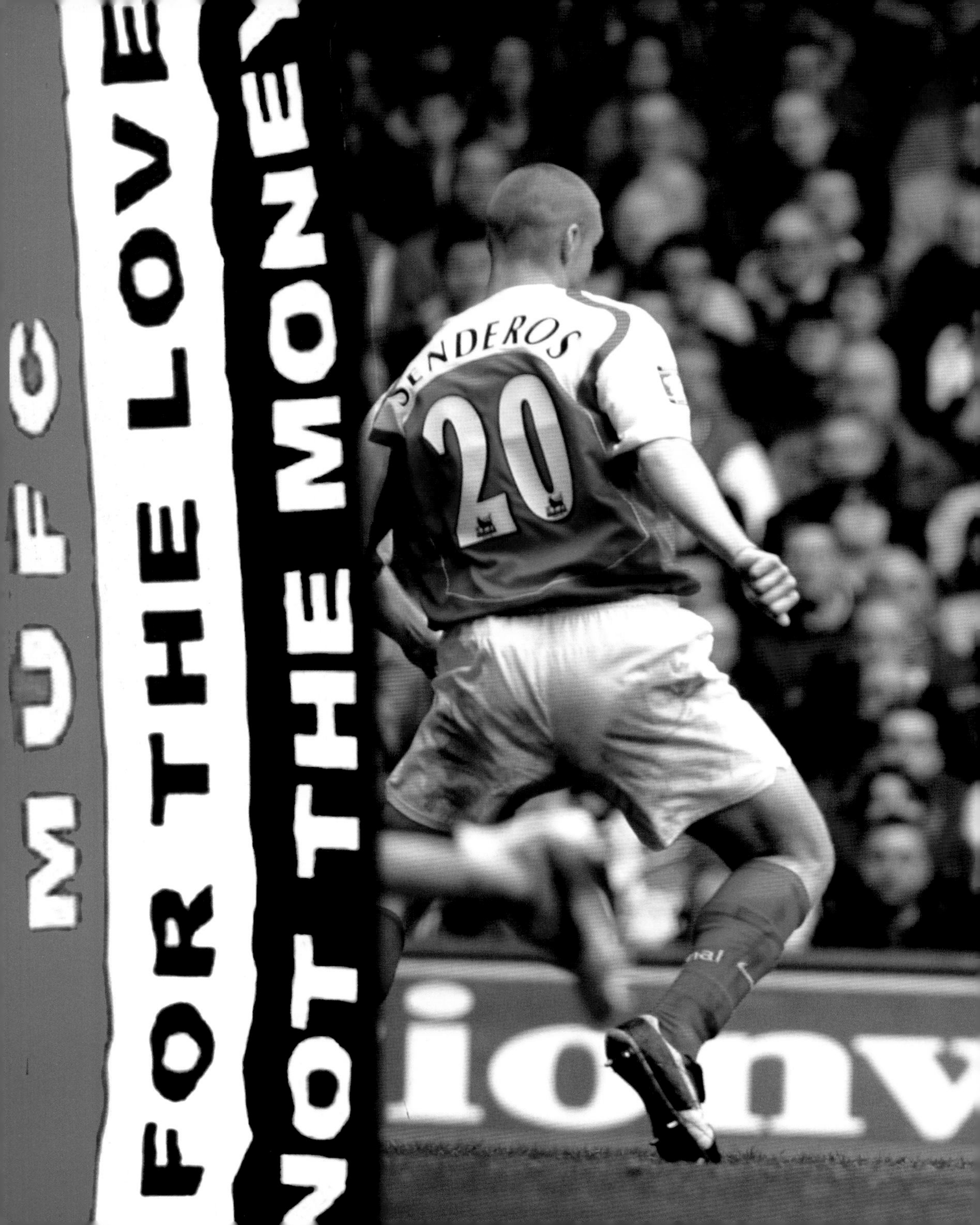
MUFC
FOR THE LOVE
NOT THE MONEY
SENDEROS
20

21st May Arsenal 0–0 Manchester United FA Cup Final 2005 (Arsenal win 5–4 on pens.)

This was another game where the twin attack of Wayne and Cristiano Ronaldo sent shudders down the spine of the best defence in the Premier League. Within minutes, United were raiding the Arsenal penalty area with Ronaldo playing down the left side like a man possessed. Rooney was marauding on the right flank and all through the match he seemed to be destined to score a goal: denied once by a post from an angle, and another time by a fine save from Lehmann. The game was a grim one for an injury-hit Arsenal side but somehow they survived the first half, then the second, and the game seemed to be moving inexorably towards penalties, even though it was the most one-sided FA Cup Final many could remember.

Arsenal even hung on with ten men when Jose Antonio Reyes lost his cool and got sent off near the end of extra time. Wenger's side, however, for once looked happy to sit back and play for penalties, while United were already looking back in frustration at the umpteen chances that had come to nothing, including a goal-line clearance from Freddie Ljungberg.

As the final whistle blew, players slumped to the floor, some to plot their penalty in a few minutes, some to have a well-earned rest. Arsenal had an awful record on penalties but it was all looking quite ominous for United having failed to take their chances during the game. Wayne and Ronaldo hit their penalties with style but of all people, it was fading United veteran Scholes who missed his. At the death, everything depended on the departing Arsenal captain Patrick Vieira. Vieira had tasted defeat in a shootout before and he was not going to miss this. As the ball hit the back of the net, the Arsenal cheers couldn't drown out the groans of disbelief in half the crowd; some United players succumbed to tears. Wayne should by rights have won himself man-of-the-match in his first Cup Final, but it had come to nothing as keeper Jens Lehmann snatched the individual award and the trophy.

Looking back on his first season gave Wayne a lot to think about. His old club had improved their lot dramatically without his input, qualifying for a Champions League place with a dour, hard-working team without stars. When he was seeing out his final days at Everton he had been criticised for playing averagely for them and brilliantly for England and, in truth, he picked up more bookings than goals at Everton. But playing with United, and under the tutulage of Fergie, he had been one of the undoubted stars of the show, scoring 17 goals in total – 11 in the Premiership, including several contenders for goal of the season.

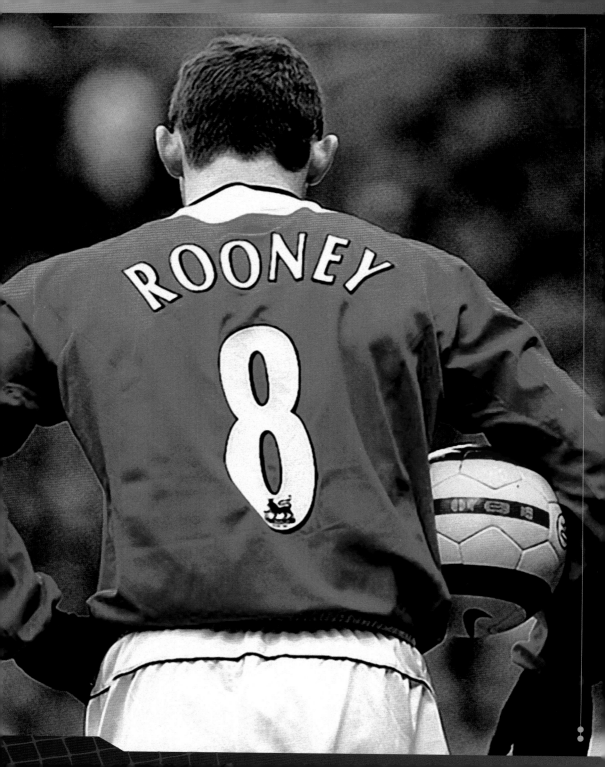

The down side of his debut season had been no trophies and the debacle in Spain. With the World Cup coming at the end of the next season, he saw honours with United and consolidating his England place as his priority. He spelled out his ambition to win both club and international honours to the **News of the World**: 'We've now gone two years without a title and the players know that's not good enough. This is a big season for us. Every player is looking to the World Cup. I think we've got every chance of winning it – it could be our year.'

The previous year, pre-season preparations were handicapped by the broken foot he sustained at Euro 2004, but he was confident he would start the new campaign in better physical shape after their Far East tour. 'I am really happy with my fitness,' he said. 'We have had three games on our tour of Asia and it has really got me going. Last year I didn't get a full pre-season because of my injuries, so this is the first time in two years I have been able to get the hard work done at this early stage.'

He also vowed to improve his disciplinary record in the season to come ahead of an England friendly with Denmark: 'Moving to United was always going to benefit me, working with the manager and the players there. I have learnt a lot and I have matured a lot, both on and off the field. I want to make sure I don't get booked for dissent. Every player does it but it gets highlighted a lot more because of who I am. I'm looking to cut out the silly bookings.

Towards the World Cup

The England friendly fixture was a disaster, Denmark turning them over 4–1 in what seemed like a freak result, but by netting a late consolation Rooney managed to extricate himself from the severest criticism. Meanwhile Manchester United launched the new Premiership season with a stylish away win against none other than Everton.

13th Aug Everton 0–2 Manchester United 2005/06 Premiership

The visitors dominated for long spells and Ruud van Nistelrooy went close twice before slotting in John O'Shea's cross two minutes before half-time. Wayne doubled the lead 27 seconds after the restart after Joseph Yobo had ludicrously rolled the ball across the penalty area into his path. He had a busy and fruitful day, ignoring the boos and tormenting former team-mate Phil Neville who had been tasked with keeping him quiet. It was the perfect start to the season, followed up by yet another strike against Newcastle, but as Manchester United launched into the Champions League qualifiers and England wobbled in their progress to the World Cup, Wayne's disciplinary nightmares came back – despite all that he had said in the close season.

7th Sept Northern Ireland 1–0 England World Cup Qualifier 2006

England played Northern Ireland in Belfast in their World Cup qualifying group in September and it became one of England's most infamous games for more reasons than Wayne. It was easily the most wretched display by any England team led by Sven Goran Eriksson, as well as his first defeat in a qualifying game. Having taken the home fixture 4–0, the assorted superstars from Chelsea, Manchester United, Arsenal and Real Madrid clearly turned up expecting to pummel the shot-shy World Cup no-hopers into the ground.

But with a new team formation and the Northern Ireland players playing like their lives depended on it England found they had no answer to the passion and ideas of players from lesser leagues. The Swedish manager looked on helplessly as his millionaire stars were outfought, outplayed and ultimately unable to respond to a sensational second-half goal by former Man Utd trainee David Healy.

England really only had one chance at goal – from Beckham – and nothing worked on the night. Also not working was the Swede's idea of alternating Wayne's play from the left and right wings rather than through the middle as he had played at Euro 2004. The frustration of this got to Wayne and he reacted badly to a tackle, earning himself a yellow card that disqualified him from the next game against Austria. Whether Rooney realised this or not, David Beckham did and he attempted to calm Wayne. Beckham, the manager, the rest of the team and, indeed, TV audiences all over the country looked on aghast as the young star told his captain to 'fuck off' and appeared to lose his head completely. He reacted as if the whole world was against him, not just the referee, and by the morning it was reported that he had told half his team to fuck off. If anything, it was worse than the petulant display against Spain.

But the fall-out from this was still being felt when he next played for Manchester United against Vilarreal in the Champions League – another game his team was expected to win. This time he was dismissed for sarcastically applauding referee Kim Milton Nielsen, the referee who had sent David Beckham off against Argentina in the 1998 World Cup, just when they needed him on the pitch to find a crucial goal from somewhere. While there was amusement at the idea that Wayne had learned the meaning of satirical intent, there were now worries that he was losing control and that the big games were tipping him over the top. It was reported that he got a apoplectic bollocking from Alex Ferguson – perhaps not before time – that seemed to set him back on the correct path.

Against a Sunderland side that were already doomed to relegation before Christmas, he gave a brilliant performance. A blistering break culminated in Wayne eluding Kelvin Davis and sliding the ball home for United's opener, and then he played in Ruud van Nistelrooy for the Dutch striker to double the lead and seal the Tynesiders' fate. Alex Ferguson has a man-management tactic of following the 'hairdryer' treatment with lavish praise: soon afterwards he compared Wayne Rooney to none other than George Best, who sadly died in the days before United's November win at West Ham.

Rooney replicated his incisive Sunderland contribution at Upton Park, scoring once and setting up another as United triumphed 2-1 in a match preceded by one minute of loud applause in honour of Best. 'I hoped somebody would produce moments in the game that reflected George Best,' said a delighted Ferguson.

'Wayne is only 20 and without question the best young player I've ever seen.'

Wayne had also been moved by the death of Best – who had praised him lavishly – stating a desire to follow in his footsteps by winning the European Cup. 'Seeing the images of George did inspire me – he was one of the best, if not the best player in the world,' said Wayne. He added, with some humility: 'I've got a long way to go before I get to that, but hopefully in the future someone will speak of me like that.' But somebody already was, with the West Ham boss Alan Pardew saying, 'Maybe he deserved to wear George Best's old number seven shirt; he was that good.'

He was at it again in a 4–0 demolition of surprise package Wigan just before Christmas, scoring twice and hitting the bar. He appeared to have lost control when he slipped inside the area, allowing Matt Jackson to make a challenge. But he quickly regained his footing – and the ball – before stepping inside Leighton Baines and rifling a low left-foot shot into the net. He didn't have to wait long for his second, as he latched on to Van Nistelrooy's pass to run clear and send a delicate chip past Pollitt – a stylish finish becoming something of a trademark.

Then he was outstanding again, this time without scoring, as United brushed aside Bolton at Old Trafford. His side were rewarded for a blistering start when Bruno N'Gotty put Kieran Richardson's cross into his own net. Bolton equalised through Gary Speed's header but United were back in front at half-time after Louis Saha slotted in a goal from close range. But United made it 3–1 when Wayne set up Cristiano Ronaldo to tap home and the Portuguese winger wrapped up the win after a mazy run. Wayne left the pitch to a standing ovation after yet another magnificent display, which meant the rested Ruud van Nistelrooy was hardly missed.

As had happened before, Wayne's temperament problems were worked through by getting his head down and playing, and the furore of the Northern Ireland game seemed a million miles away as Ferguson tipped Wayne Rooney to be a future captain of the club after Roy Keane (no stranger to a temper-tantrum himself) suddenly upped and left the club in some acrimony. Ferguson handed the skipper's role to Gary Neville after Roy Keane's exit but suggested that the 20-year-old may be next in line.

*'I think we may have a potential captain in Wayne Rooney,' he told the **Sunday Mirror**. 'I think there are indications he has the mental toughness, respect and the winning mentality.'*

Perhaps Ferguson was thinking of the way the responsibility of captaincy had calmed and inspired Eric Cantona when he'd drop-kicked a Crystal Palace supporter in 1995 after being sent off.

But unfortunately for Wayne, Ferguson and United, the season was unravelling. Although they earned a creditable victory against Chelsea, the London side were again unreachable thanks to the size of the squad – the money that Ferguson had spent on Wayne alone could have bought five players and he was working on more limited resources than ever. This fact told in the Champions League where injury problems hampered their chances. United's failure to score against Vilarreal in either group game cost them dear, and Rooney's self-inflicted suspension did not help matters. For the first time since 1995/96, United had failed to reach the knockout stage of Europe's premier competition.

26th February Manchester United 4–0 Wigan Carling Cup Final 2005/06

To make matters worse, hated rivals and newly-crowned European Champions Liverpool had knocked them out of the FA Cup. But Ferguson was not one to deny his players a trophy – and Wayne's first came in the consolation form of the Carling League Cup. Wayne returned to Cardiff, the setting of one of his greatest unrewarded displays in the match against Arsenal, and he showed the hallmarks of a great player by providing an improved action replay. As in the FA Cup final, he was soon smacking the woodwork, and showed himself once more to be a tireless runner and immense presence. But this time he made sure he got himself on the scoresheet.

Edwin Van der Sar's long punt downfield was flicked on by Saha, and defenders Arjan De Zeeuw and Pascal Chimbonda collided to leave Wayne with a clear run on goal to slot clinically past Filan on 33 minutes. Saha added another in the second half and almost immediately set up Ronaldo for a third.

A gutsy Wigan side were simply outclassed, conceding the same scoreline as they had at Old Trafford. The fourth came from Rooney again when he spinned away from his marker in the area and finished beautifully. It was a fitting end to another man-of-the-match display and this time he was officially recognised as such, picking up the champagne along with his first cup winner's medal.

With apparently nothing left to play for in the season, the pressure was off United and while Chelsea began to cruise the Reds put together a run of Championship-winning form. Having hit a league run of no goals in January and February, without a noticeable dipping-off in form, Rooney the striker hit back with a vengeance in March and April, starting with yet another brace against poor old Newcastle. He followed this up with goals in wins against Birmingham, Arsenal again, and two more to see off Champions League hopefuls Spurs. Nine straight wins saw United leapfrog Liverpool as Chelsea's nearest rivals and suddenly, with five games to go including a Chelsea v United 'six-pointer', it was just about conceivable that the Red Devils could go even better than their 1995/96 pursuit of Newcastle and complete a remarkable Championship turnaround!

Alas, it was fantasy as a 'it just wouldn't go in' goalless draw at home to long relegated Sunderland put the kibosh on that. Meanwhile Chelsea came back from 0–1 down with ten men to see off West Ham 4–1 and then followed up with a convincing win at Bolton, which meant the 'six-pointer' at Stamford Bridge was academic. At least a win would stop Chelsea holding their celebration party right in front of their noses. Ferguson ponted out that a result would also lay down something of a marker to a slightly stale Chelsea side for next season.

What followed was the exact opposite, and the most distressing day in the 20-year-old life of Wayne Rooney. Bad enough was to go 1–0 down to a soft goal from William Gallas after a poorly-defended set-piece with five minutes on the clock. Worse still was to wriggle, fight and then suddenly gloriously accelerate past the last blue defender to find himself through on goal, only to surprise everybody in the stadium by scuffing his shot wide when one-on-one with Petr Cech.

With another powerful low 25-yarder kept out by the Chelsea stopper, it looked like even an unusually subdued Wayne represented United's only chance of keeping the title race alive. But, in the second half, Chelsea rubbed salt in the wound by going 3–0 up with two fabulous goals, a Joe Cole stunner that seemed to bode well for England's chances in the imminent World Cup, and a fine team goal that ended with Cole setting up the overlapping centre-back Ricardo Carvalho to hammer home.

For United it was all too reminiscent of Tony Adams' marauding goal in the 4-0 win over Everton that settled Arsenal's comeback championship in 1997/98, another bad memory they could do without. It was certainly too much for Wayne Rooney, who got himself booked for his second silly late challenge of the game. Alex Ferguson looked like he'd seen enough, and with ten minutes to go he was looking to bring on defender Patrice Evra, possibly at the expense of the tiring talisman before he got himself sent off again. Rooney had already been involved in an early 50-50 clash with Chelsea captain John Terry, where a slightly raised foot had left his England colleague limping bravely through the game while Sven-Goran Eriksson looked on nervously.

But far worse was to come. Setting off on one final run towards the area before his number came up, from the same left-hand side where he had done so much damage for England, he was tackled by Paulo Ferreira and fell. The fans groaned when he rolled around in the area clutching his right foot, it looked like a pantomime attempt to get a free kick or a sending off when the challenge had been perfectly fair. But then it dawned, this was Wayne Rooney we were talking about here: not some fragile foreign showboat with no stomach for the fight. Sub Ruud van Nistelrooy had both hands in the air almost immediately pleading for a stoppage. If Wayne Rooney stayed down, it meant he was hurt.

England colleagues on both sides crowded round with their hands on their heads or over their mouths. The party atmosphere in Stamford Bridge, as Chelsea looked forward to celebrating at the final whistle, changed markedly as fans in all colours realised England's summer was on the line. Suddenly United's problems were everyone's problems.

Four agonising minutes later Wayne Rooney completed his substitution on an orange stretcher. The chant went up from the fans: 'There goes our World Cup.' His season was certainly over, but the question on everybody's lips would be fit for June? Early word from the dressing room was mixed: not as bad as first thought, came one theory. Upstairs the press boxes were full of contradictory rumours, ranging from a dead leg to broken ankle. What was certain was that Wayne had landed awkwardly, looked in tears as he lay on the pitch and medics had removed his shoe. Later he was seen hobbling onto the team coach with crutches.

Later in the evening club doctors confirmed, if not the very worst fears, then at least the words everyone had been dreading. 'Wayne Rooney has fractured the base of the fourth metatarsal on the right foot and he will be out for six weeks,' said a short statement. The World Cup kick-off was almost exactly six weeks to the day; it was too tight to bear thinking about. This was the bone next to the one he had cracked in Euro 2004, which meant a 10-week lay-off before he played again.

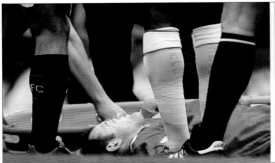

images (c) reuters

Even Mourinho was quick to offer words of pity: **'England need the boy, the World Cup needs the boy,'** he said. In fact the whole of football was soon lining up to sign the book of condolence. It is a mark of the spectacular impression he had made that pundits who had made England second-favourites behind Brazil for the trophy were now writing off their chances. No less a judge than Steven Gerrard, voted Europe's most valuable player of the previous year, declared it would be 'impossible to have a successful World Cup without Wayne Rooney', and this seemed to be the cry from every fan. Don't forget, this is only a twenty-year-old we are talking about.

Perhaps it was too much pressure to place on young shoulders anyway: remember Ronaldo in 1998, remember Beckham in the same year. England have other players who on form might make the difference – Beckham himself, Gerrard, Joe Cole, Owen, Lampard – but this was the first World Cup since 1990 that England were to go into with a bona fide genius in the squad. Maybe it will turn out for the best. Maybe the team will learn to play together rather than rely on one man, make it through the group, and welcome back a rampaging teenage super-sub from the knockout stages onwards (just remember what happened when he returned from his last metatarsal injury, against Fenerbahce). Or maybe, sadly, the world audience will be denied the only player who compares with Ronaldinho in terms of expectations in this competition.

Will he travel? Sir Alex Ferguson thinks not. And as a true Scot, and a United manager with so much resting on his long-term fitness, perhaps he hopes not. Either way, he claims he will have the final say, aggravated by Eriksson's insistence that, in the case of his one truly unique player, the normal rules don't apply. He has said he would take him if there was any chance of him featuring at any stage, and FIFA – eager to get the best audiences and the best spectacle – agree. They have stated that Eriksson has special dispensation until June 9th, two days before England's first group game against Paraguay, to call in a replacement. A replacement for the irreplaceable.

The medical consensus is that predictions are unreliable, but the sunshine scenario would see Rooney miss the opening group games but return somewhere between the Sweden match and the quarter-finals, should England get there without him. The grandest stage would then be set for a spectacular comeback... but remember how David Beckham came back too early from the same injury in 2002, and how the team suffered as a result.

How have the hopes of so many come to rest on an under-21 player with a suspect temperament and a dodgy foot? Well, just watch him on the pitch. Just enjoy the matchless show-reel of great goals he has already scored, count the man-of-the-match awards he won as a teenager, all those games he looked like he'd win on his own by scaring the life out of the opposition every time he touched the ball. With Rooney requiring three or four markers to stop him whenever he runs on goal or hits the flanks, he spares his team-mates the close attentions of defenders: that's why his England colleagues want him on the pitch whatever it takes. Although United's second League Cup win represents a poor return on two seasons of excellence at the world's most famous club, Wayne Rooney is already on his way to establishing himself as one of Manchester United's greatest players. His form in United colours has been a considerable consolation to their success-starved fans since joining in 2004 and these displays are still fresh in the memory of every England fan.

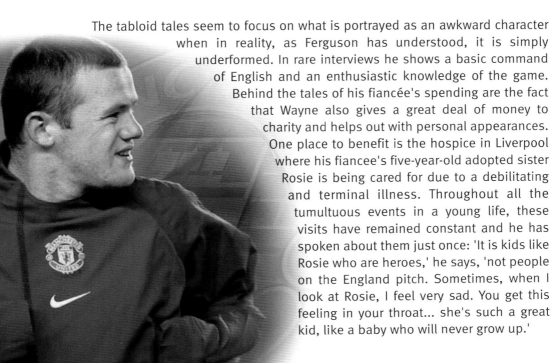

The tabloid tales seem to focus on what is portrayed as an awkward character when in reality, as Ferguson has understood, it is simply underformed. In rare interviews he shows a basic command of English and an enthusiastic knowledge of the game. Behind the tales of his fiancée's spending are the fact that Wayne also gives a great deal of money to charity and helps out with personal appearances. One place to benefit is the hospice in Liverpool where his fiancee's five-year-old adopted sister Rosie is being cared for due to a debilitating and terminal illness. Throughout all the tumultuous events in a young life, these visits have remained constant and he has spoken about them just once: 'It is kids like Rosie who are heroes,' he says, 'not people on the England pitch. Sometimes, when I look at Rosie, I feel very sad. You get this feeling in your throat... she's such a great kid, like a baby who will never grow up.'

Even now, Wayne himself is being treated to a great extent 'like a baby who will never grow up,' but perhaps this insight into his private life will focus our minds on the fact that there are things bigger than football.

Meanwhile Eriksson clings to Wayne's medical bulletins like a child to its comfort rag. But Ferguson is right to insist that it will be Manchester United – that is, Fergie – not Eriksson who decides whether or not Rooney is fit enough to go to the 2006 World Cup.

But there here will be other World Cups for Wayne Rooney, maybe three more at his absolute peak; there will be other Euro Championships, other Cup Finals at home and abroad, and surely a Champions League trophy. There seems little doubt he will be involved on football's greatest stages for years to come. He is destined to become one of the greats of the game: he will be up there with Pelé, Best, Cruyff, Maradona, Zidane...

And there is always the hope that against all the odds he will make it to Germany, against that there is the certainty that one day...

England will win a World Cup with Wayne Rooney pulling the strings and the trigger.

But Wayne is beginning to show a wry sense of humour. When he was asked who England will now use up front in Germany. He offered a couple of name, then added:

'Of course we have others, like Peter Crouch...if he starts to play.'

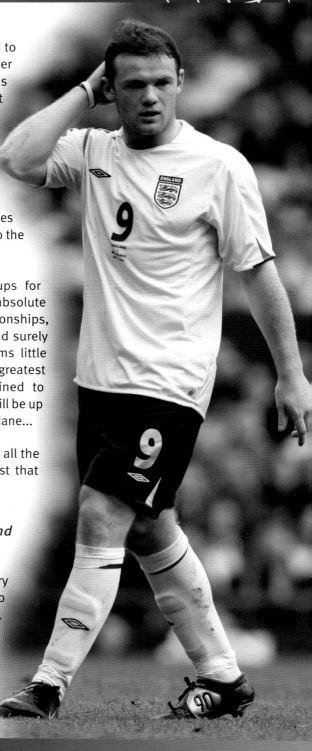